Simply Healthy

NO ADDED SUGAR, SALT, FATS
LOW CHOLESTEROL COOKING

Pritikin-style cooking

by

Suzanne Porter

DAVID & CHARLES
Newton Abbot   London

Cover photograph: Mushroom souffle pie (RD) (page 58), Cannelloni (RD) (page 63), Broccoli and cauliflower mornay (RD) (page 55), fresh fruit (RD), iced water

Moist plain chestnut cake (RD) (page 100) with creamy chestnut frosting (RD) topped with roasted sprouts (RD).

British Library Cataloguing in Publication Data

Porter, Suzanne
   Simply healthy : no added sugar, salt, fats,
   low cholesterol cooking : Pritikin-style cooking.
   1. Cookery (Natural foods)
   I. Title
   641.5'637   TX741

ISBN 0-7153-9006-6

© Suzanne & Gordon Porter 1986, 1987

All rights reserved. No part of this
publication may be reproduced, stored
in a retrieval system, or transmitted,
in any form or by any means, electronic,
mechanical, photocopying, recording or
otherwise, without the prior permission
of David & Charles Publishers plc

Photography by Phil Wymant, Latrobe Studios
Typeset by ProComp Productions Pty Ltd, South Australia
and printed in Great Britain
by Redwood Burn Ltd, Trowbridge, Wiltshire
for David & Charles Publishers plc
Brunel House   Newton Abbot   Devon

Dedication

To the memory of Nathan Pritikin, a man of great courage who dared to tell the Western world that its diet is the cause of degenerative diseases, who encouraged the Western world to change to a dietary lifestyle based on whole grains, fresh vegetables and fruit. This diet will not only improve your health, but it will also offer a longer life, reducing the risks of developing degenerative diseases such as heart disease, hypertension, mature onset diabetes, arthritis and some cancers — these diseases we take for granted that we will develop as we age.

Nathan Pritikin brought hope and health to many thousands of grateful people. He will be remembered as the foremost dietary reformer of our time and his great work will continue.

Acknowledgements

Gordon and I wish to thank Roma and Donna who somehow managed to understand the writing and helped with the typing; Super Sprouts of Flinders, Victoria, who provided the roasted sprouts to decorate the chestnut cake; and a special thanks to Lorraine Lynas, Marjorie Bowditch, my sister, Wallace Thorpe, and my mother, Hazel Proctor, for their help with the photographic session.

Suzanne Porter

Contents

Preface	8
Foreword	9
The diet	11
Soups	37
Salads	45
Vegetables	53
Meat, poultry and fish	69
Desserts	81
Cakes and slices	93
Bread, scones and pastries	101
Spreads, chutneys and pastes	113
Dips, dressings and sauces	119
Beverages	127
Index	131

Preface

I began to use the Pritikin programme about fourteen months after I was diagnosed in 1980 as having osteo-arthritis in my left hip joint.

At the age of 46 this diagnosis was devastating to me — I was lame, in constant pain, taking medication and very depressed. I was still working full-time as a nursing sister.

Then I chanced to read an article about Nathan Pritikin and his work with patients who had degenerative diseases such as hypertension, coronary artery disease, mature diabetes, obesity, atheroselenosis, angina, hypoglycaemia and arthritis and whose health improved when they went off the Western diet and on to his 10 per cent fat diet and exercise programme.

Because my family and I have experienced excellent health since we began this programme in 1981, we take no medication. I have no pain, my limp is gone, and I run and exercise every day.

I feel I want to help as many people as possible. My first book, *It's Only Natural*, has indeed helped many hundreds of people and, because of this, I have experimented further in my kitchen and compiled more recipes to expand the Pritikin kitchen even further.

Many thousands of people in Australia are now responding to scientific evidence that the Western diet is unhealthy by changing their lifestyles. This is extremely encouraging.

I have endeavoured to explain very simply how to start the programme and how to follow both the Maintenance and Regression Diets. Since there has been some confusion over which foods are allowed and which are not, I have tried to make this as clear as possible.

I have once again indicated on each recipe either 'MD' for Maintenance Diet or 'RD' for Regression Diet. In order to remain faithful to either of these diets, it is important to choose recipes strictly according to this code.

I wish you all good luck, happy cooking the new way and, most of all, good health.

Suzanne Porter

Foreword

Most people getting started on the Pritikin Programme want, more than anything else, basic, practical advice on planning, purchasing and preparing their new food. Suzanne Porter's excellent cookbooks, *It's Only Natural* and *Simply Healthy*, are the answer to this need. Straightforward and easy to follow, they set out a host of tasty suggestions that are strictly in accordance with Pritikin's scientifically sound and successful principles. By firmly adopting these, more and more people all over the world are finding renewed health and vigour.

Suzanne Porter's arthritis promptly ceased to worry her when she changed to a Pritikin diet but soon recurs if she transgresses. This has taught her the importance of following the guidelines strictly. This necessity has also been demonstrated to me by the experience of hundreds of patients whose problems were resolved only when they corrected a casual following of these principles to a precise one.

Good food should taste good and be a delight in its presentation, as well as being good for us. Here the skill and ingenuity of our Australian cooks has come to our aid with a run of best-selling health cooking guides which now lead the world in making healthy natural food look and taste 'gourmet'. *Simply Healthy* is one of the best in this field. It does not confuse the beginner by including ingredients outside Pritikin's recommendations as many of the other cookbooks do.

I applaud Suzanne's latest book and know it will lead its readers to much eating enjoyment, at the same time confounding those sceptics who doubt that really healthy food can taste delicious as well.

L. H. McMahon, MB, BS, FRCSI, FRCS(Edin.)
President of the Pritikin Lifestyle Association

The diet

This diet is high in complex carbohydrates and fibre, and low in fat and cholestrol.

You will now be eating:

Complex carbohydrates 80 per cent of your food intake.
Protein 10 to 15 per cent of your food intake.
Fat and cholesterol 5 to 10 per cent of your food intake.

Well, you have decided to change your lifestyle and have read the relevant books but are not quite sure how to start the programme. These introductory pages are to help you get started — to help you make the transition from the Western diet a little more easily. I hope that they will also encourage you to persevere with the change in lifestyle and make it as easy as possible.

I will explain the most important aspects of the programme, but this information in no way substitutes for the programme books.

First, a change in lifestyle includes a change in eating habits, complete with a sensible exercise programme. This change in lifestyle is intended to improve your health and to make an improvement to any degenerative disease. It will also reduce the risk of developing degenerative diseases as you age.

There are two versions of the diet: the Regression Diet and the Maintenance Diet.

- The Regression Diet is a simple diet aimed at avoiding cholesterol and minimizing the intake of fat, oil, and animal protein.
- The Maintenance Diet, on the other hand, allows a little more animal protein (about 630 g of lean meat, fish, and poultry per week), a little extra fruit, and limited quantities of dried fruit.

Each of these diets and the foods acceptable are explained in my book *It's Only Natural*.

Warning: It is advisable when considering any dietary change to first consult a doctor who is familiar with the Pritikin Program, particularly if you are taking medication. The doctor will be able to monitor your condition and will reduce your medication according to your response. Do not, however, attempt to do this on your own, as this could be quite dangerous to your health.

Suggested reference books

Live Longer Now (Australian edition) by Jon N. Leonard, J. I. Holfer and N. Pritikin, Lansdowne Press, Sydney, 1974.

The Pritikin Program for Diet and Exercise by Nathan Pritikin and Patrick M. McGrady Jr, Schwartz, East Melbourne, 1979.

The Pritikin Permanent Weight Loss Manual by Nathan Pritikin, Bantam Books, Sydney, 1982.

The Pritikin Promise: 28 days to a Longer Life by Nathan Pritikin, Bantam Books, Sydney, 1983.

Cooking book

It's Only Natural: No added sugar, salt, fats and low cholesterol cooking by Suzanne Porter, Greenhouse, Richmond, Victoria, 1985.

Regression and Maintenance Diets — permissible amounts

Dairy foods

Liquid skim milk, 1 per cent fat maximum.
Both diets: 1 cup.
Non-fat yoghurt, 1 per cent fat maximum.
Both diets: less than ¼ cup.
Evaporated skim milk, 1 per cent fat maximum.
Both diets: 120 g per day.   2 servings maximum per day.
Non-fat (skim) milk powder, 1 per cent fat maximum.
Both diets: 5 tablespoons or 1 serving.
Low fat skim milk cottage cheese, 1 per cent fat maximum.
Both diets: 60 g or 1 serving.
Sapsago or Geska cheese.
Both diets: 30 g to 60 g maximum per week.

Fats and oils

This includes saturated, unsaturated, and polyunsaturated butter and margarine, cold pressed oil, olive oil, corn oil, peanut oil, safflower oil, lard, suet and coconut oil.
Both diets: nil.

Fibre

This is the part of the plant which is not digested and is found in grains, fruit and vegetables and unprocessed bran.
  Remember: meat, dairy products, white flour and white bread have no fibre.
Both diets: plenty of fibre is encouraged.

Meat, poultry and fish

Both diets: see section 'Meat, Poultry and Fish Choices'.

Eggs

Whites only. Egg yolks contain around 280 g of cholesterol in *each* yolk and are therefore not included in this programme. This includes fish eggs, caviar, shad roe etc.
Both diets: 7 whites per week maximum.

Salt

Salt may be either sodium or potassium.
Both diets: nil.

Starches (complex carbohydrates)

Starches take longer to metabolize, burn 100 per cent clean and convert into energy. They are found in grains, fruit and vegetables.

Grains—whole or lightly milled grains, for example, oats, buckwheat, barley, triticale, rye, brown rice, wheat, stoneground wholemeal plain flour, unbleached white plain flour, unprocessed bran, millet, corn, sago.

Approved Pritikin commercial bread is now obtainable at supermarkets and health food stores. If in doubt use my recipe for bread in the 'Bread, Scones and Pastries' section of this book. Read labels carefully before purchasing bread, pitas, pasta, spaghetti, etc. Make sure it is:

Pita breads (wholemeal)   all made without
Pasta (wholemeal)   sugar, salt, fat and
Spaghetti (wholemeal)   oils.

Both diets: wheat germ is not permitted but all other grains are acceptable in unlimited quantities.

Fruit — means all fruit except that which is prepared commercially with sweetener, eg. jams, honey, syrup, preserved fruit. If triglycerides are above 125 mg eat only fresh fruit in permitted amounts.

Use unsweetened apple juice concentrate in small amounts, 3 g maximum per day to sweeten dishes.

Maintenance Diet: 5 pieces of unsweetened fresh or canned fruit maximum per day. Always eat 1 piece of citrus fruit out of this ration.

Regression Diet: 3 pieces of fresh fruit maximum per day. Always eat 1 piece of citrus fruit out of this ration.

Vegetables — all vegetables except olives and avocados.
Both diets: unlimited quantities except olives and avocados.

Herbs and spices

See section 'Herbs and Spices'.

Sugars (simple carbohydrates)

These raise blood sugar levels and triglyceride levels and must be avoided. (*Triglycerides* burn with exercise.) Sugars do not curb the appetite. Sugars include honey, molasses, golden syrup, malt extract, treacle, raw and refined sugar (all colours) including icing sugar, coffee sugar, brown sugar, cubed sugar, fructose, dextrose, sucrose, and commercial products containing sugar of any kind. Artificial sweeteners are not recommended.
Both diets: nil.

Beans and lentils

All beans and peas except soybeans and tofu (soybean curd) may be used, unless substituted for the meat allowances — see section 'Meat, Poultry and Fish Choices'.

Soy beans and tofu (soybean curd)

Maintenance Diet: If you eat 90 g maximum once per week it will replace your entire daily allowance of meat, poultry and fish on that day.
Regression Diet: 90 g maximum serving *once* per week *only*.

Cereals

Rolled oats, home made muesli (made from approved cereals), mixed rolled grains, and cracked wheat may be used.

Be very careful to read the labels on commercially prepared cereals. It is wiser to eat home prepared combinations of allowable grains.

Remember: Wheat germ is not allowed in your programme.
Both diets: unlimited quantities, unless you are reducing your weight.

Sprouted seeds and grains

See section 'Sprouting, Seeds, Legumes and Grains'.
Both diets: unlimited.

Nuts

See section 'Nuts and Seeds'.
Both diets: with the exception of chestnuts, nil.

Seeds

See section 'Nuts and Seeds'.
Both diets: with the exception of sesame, poppy, celery, mustard and caraway seeds, nil.

Dried fruit

Always buy and use natural sun dried fruit (it is always very dark in colour and dry): for example, natural raisins, natural sultanas, undipped currants, sun dried figs, sun dried apricots (soak to reconstitute) and natural dates.

Always wash and dry the fruit carefully. Most sun dried fruit should be soaked in water and drained before usage; this softens and reconstitutes it.
Maintenance Diet: 30 g maximum per day.
Regression diet: nil.

Cakes and Puddings

I have experimented for many hours to produce cakes and puddings that are reasonably acceptable. It should always be remembered when eating cakes and puddings that portions should be small and kept within the Pritikin guidelines.
Maintenance Diet: You may use all the cake and pudding recipes in both of my books, remembering to keep the dried fruit intake to 30 g.
Regression Diet: I have experimented with recipes and have included recipes for several cakes and slices that are suitable to eat. Be careful, however, not to use the recipes that contain dried fruit or which have the sign 'MD' beside them (see recipes in 'Cakes and Slices' section).

Herbal teas and approved grain beverages

Both diets: as desired.

Fruit juices

These must be unsweetened (with no added sugar).
Maintenance Diet: 226 g maximum per week.
Regression diet: nil.

Vegetable juices

Vegetable juices must have no added salt or sugar.
Both diets: 2 glasses maximum per week.

Wines for cooking only

Dry white wine   must always be used as a flavouring and
Cooking sherry   be cooked in the recipe.
Brandy
Whisky
Both diets: limited use.

Spreads

Preferably use only home made spreads. Follow recipes in *It's Only Natural* (in section 'Sauces, Gravies, Toppings, and Spreads') and in this book (in section 'Spreads, Chutneys and Pastes'). There are now some commercially prepared spreads available which are made without sugar or artificial sweeteners — read labels carefully.
Both diets: use sparingly.

Sauces

Use only home made sauces according to strict Pritikin guidelines. See recipes in *It's Only Natural* (in section 'Sauces, Gravies, Toppings, and Spreads') and in this book (in section 'Dips, Dressings and Sauces').
  Soy sauce (low salt) is permitted in small amounts as a flavouring. No commercial product with fat, oil, salt or sugar is allowed.
Both diets: moderate use.

Salad dressings

Use only home made dressings according to strict Pritikin guidelines. See recipes in *It's Only Natural* (in section 'Sauces, Gravies, Toppings, and Spreads') and in this book (in section 'Dips, Dressings and Sauces').
  No commercial product with fat, oil, salt or sugar is allowed.
Both diets: use according to dairy food allowances.

Gravies

See recipes in *It's Only Natural* (in section 'Sauces, Gravies, Toppings, and Spreads').
  No commercial product with fat, oil, salt or sugar is allowed.
Both diets: moderate use.

Suggestion for a day's eating

You should be eating 6 to 8 small meals per day. Eat something from the food allowance about every 2 hours during the day. This will also curb your appetite if you are on a weight loss programme and will maintain a steady blood sugar level which is neither high or low.

Breakfast	Cereal
	Skim milk liquid
	A piece of citrus fruit
	Approved grain beverage and skim milk
Mid-morning	Home made scone or pita bread and salad vegetables
Lunch	Vegetable soup
	Salad with sprouted grains
	Banana
Mid-afternoon	Hot vegetables or salad
4 pm	Slice of approved cake
	Approved grain beverage and skim milk
Dinner	Soup
	Main meal: vegetable or meat casserole according to whichever diet you adopt.
	Piece of fruit
Supper	Sandwich of approved bread and filling according to whichever diet you adopt.
	Approved grain beverage and skim milk

Read labels carefully—look for:

- No added sugar
- No added salt
- No fat or oil
- No preservatives, artificial flavourings or colourings.
- Buy unwaxed apples and oranges and do not use waxed orange peel in cooking.
- Try to buy organically grown fruit and vegetables.
- Try to buy free range poultry and eggs (use the whites only).

Foods permitted on this programme

I will list as many of the foods permitted on this programme as I am aware of. You may find there are some that I have missed and that they are your favourites. If so, then use them providing they are from the permissible categories.

Whole grains

Barley, both pearl and unpearled
Bran, unprocessed
Brown rice, normal and biodynamic
Buckwheat (low in gluten)
Bulga wheat (Kasha)
Burghul (Lebanese cracked wheat), Tabouli
Corn, cornmeal (Polenta), cornflour (There is a cornflour made from wheat that is acceptable, but not if you are allergic to wheat products.)
Lebanese bread (wholemeal), also called pita bread
Millet, whole or hulled
Oats rolled (oatmeal, ground)
Rice flakes
Rye, both flour and flakes
Sago
Tapioca
Triticale flakes or (stoneground) flour
Unbleached flour
Wheat flakes
Wholemeal (stoneground) flour both self raising and plain

Many of the grains including wheat, oats, rye, brown rice and barley are now available in flaked or kibbled form. This makes them easier to use for bread making, cake making and adding to muesli.

Gluten

If a 'gluten allergy' exists, then more use should be made of non-gluten grains.
Gluten grains — wheat, oats, barley and rye.
Non-gluten grains — corn (maize), millet and brown rice.
Low gluten — buckwheat.

Dried legumes

Beans — for example, black, brown, garbanzo (chick peas), red, pinto, calico and lima. (Use beans sparingly because they have a high protein content.)
Continental Soup Mix (health store item) — a mixture of beans, lentils and grains

Nuts and seeds

Because the fat/oil content of nuts and seeds is so high, you may only use chestnuts, fresh or dried.
Sesame seeds may only be used as a garnish or topping on cakes and some dishes.
Poppy seeds may also be used as a garnish or topping.
Celery, mustard and caraway seeds may be used sparingly in salads.

Lentils

Whole or split varieties.
Peas, split, as well as yellow and green.
Lentil Pea Soup mix (health store item).

Vegetables

Artichokes
Asparagus
Beans, green, yellow and purple
Beetroot
Broccoli
Brussel sprouts
Cabbage, both green, curly
  leaf and red
Carrots
Cauliflower
Celery
Chives
Corn kernels
Cucumbers
Egg plant (Aubergine,
  nightshade)
Endive
Garlic, fresh or commercially
  prepared, without salt
Leeks
Lettuce, both green and brown
  (all varieties)
Marrow
Mushrooms, field and
  commercially grown, button
Onions, spring, white, salad,
  brown and pickling
Parsnips
Peas
Peppers (Capsicums), red and
  green (nightshade)
Potatoes (nightshade)
Pumpkin
Radishes
Silver beet
Squash
Swede
Sweet Potatoes
Tomatoes, all varieties including
  cherry (nightshade)
Turnips
Watercress
Zucchini

Avocados and olives are not included in your programme due to their high fat/oil content.

If you are concerned about the very low fat/oil intake in this programme, it is worth noting that there is a certain amount of fat/oil in the make-up of all the above mentioned foods. It is therefore impossible not to eat fat/oil in a natural form in this programme. Of course, the best source of fat/oil is from vegetable origin not animal.

If you are using canned vegetables try to buy those that are processed without added sugar or salt, and preferably those with no artificial colouring, flavouring, preservatives or additives.

Remember: Except for peas and beans there is no restriction on the liberal use of the above mentioned grains and vegetables.

Fruit

Apples, all varieties
Apricots
Bananas
Blackberries
Blueberries
Boysenberries

Cantaloup
Cherries
Citrus, for example, oranges, lemons and grapefruit (one serving each day)
Custard apples
Figs
Grapes, all varieties both green and black
Kiwi fruit
Loganberries
Lychees
Mangoes
Melons, watermelon, honeydew, cantaloup
Nectarines
Passionfruit
Pawpaws
Peaches
Pears
Pineapple
Plums
Raspberries
Strawberries
Tamarillos
Tangerines

It is important to note that eating large quantities of fruit may raise your triglyceride level, therefore only 3 pieces of fruit may be eaten daily on the Regression Diet and 5 pieces of fruit may be eaten daily on the Maintenance Diet.

Dried fruit

Dates
Natural raisins
Natural sultanas
Undipped currants
Prunes
Natural (Sun)-dried apricots, peaches, figs, bananas

Dried fruit is *not* permitted on the Regression Diet and only about 30 g maximum is permitted on the Maintenance Diet.

Sun-dried fruits are very dark in colour and are not dipped in sulphur.

Milk products

Milk products *must* be non-fat or 1 per cent fat maximum.

Skim milk powder
Yoghurt, non-fat, sugar free
Yoghurt, 1 per cent fat maximum, with fruit, in commercial variety
Evaporated skim milk (canned), 0·5 per cent fat content
Cottage cheese, low fat, 1 per cent fat maximum
Ricotta cheese, low fat, 1 per cent fat maximum
Geska cheese, low fat grated herb cheese
Eggs, whites only may be used, discard yolks

Beverages

Coffee substitutes made from grains are acceptable providing they are caffeine-free.

Tea substitutes are acceptable providing they are caffeine-free, for example, linden tea, rose hip tea.

Carob is a substitute for chocolate. It is made from the ground, roasted pods of the carob bean tree and in Biblical times was known as St John's bread powder. It has a high level of natural fruit sugars, and contains minerals and proteins.

Fruit and vegetable juices are acceptable providing they are sugar- and salt-free and contain no artificial colourings, flavourings, preservatives or additives. Only very small amounts of fruit juices are permitted, since over-consumption will raise triglyceride levels.

Pasta

Spaghetti (wholemeal)
Macaroni (wholemeal)
Noodles (wholemeal)
Vermicelli (wholemeal)

Always ensure that the packet states 'wholemeal' and that it is free from artificial colourings, flavourings, egg yolk and additives.

Use as the main ingredient of your favourite pasta dish or add to soups — use limited quantities if low calorie (kj) soup is required.

Flavourings

Active dry yeast
Arrowroot
Capers
Cider vinegar
Dry white wine cooked in the food
Gelatin
Herbs and spices (see separate section)
Horseradish
Lemon juice
Matso meal
Seeds and legumes (see separate section)
Soy sauce, low salt
Tabasco sauce
Tomato paste, preferably salt free
Vinegar
Wine vinegar

These may be used in small quantities to add flavour, dash or texture to a dish.

Meat, Poultry and Fish Choices

Red meat Lean round beef, with all skin and fat removed, is the recommended red meat.
100 g contains: 90 mg cholesterol; 73 g fat

Chicken or turkey White meat preferred, skin and fat removed. (Free range if possible.)
Chicken—100 g contains: 87 mg cholesterol; 49 g fat
Turkey—100 g contains: 76 mg cholesterol; 38 g fat

Seafood If you use any of these, 45 g replaces the entire daily allowance of meat, poultry or fish.
Oysters
Scallops
Mussels
Clams
Squid

Fish

Tuna Choose water-packed or in brine.
Salmon, pink
Trout 100 g of fish contains: cholesterol ranging from 34 mg to 87 mg; fat content ranging from 3 g to 40 g.
Sole
Flounder
Red snapper
Sea bass

Maintenance Diet: allows 100 g maximum per day of either meat, poultry or fish.
Regression Diet: allows 100 g maximum per week. Those with high cholesterol levels should avoid *all* meat allowances entirely. *Remember:* cholesterol wil not burn with exercise.

Note:

Lamb Fat and cholesterol levels are far too high for safe consumption and must be avoided.
Veal
T-bone steak
Sardines, oil-packed
Fish, oil-packed
Pork

Shrimp, prawns, lobster, crab — Although some of these seafoods are very high in cholesterol, the body may be able to cope with them better. Remember that 45 g replaces the entire daily or weekly meat, poultry or fish allowance depending on which diet you are following.

Taking into account the cholesterol levels of all meat, poultry and fish it would be safer to eat fish than any of the other 'meat' dishes.

Herbs and spices

Herbs and spices are used as desired to add flavour to your dishes. Taste may vary from one person to another and so herbs and spices should be used conservatively until the exact flavours are known. It is quite possible to destroy a favourite dish with their incorrect use.

Commercially prepared herbs are readily available but many people are now growing their own in pots and plots all over the country. It is possible to dry and prepare your own herbs or use them fresh from the garden.

Herbs — derive from an aromatic plant whose leaves are used to flavour food. They may be fresh or dried and are either home grown or from commercial sources.

Spices — are aromatic substances from dried bark, roots, buds and seeds and are used in food as a flavouring.

Condiment — is a seasoning or mixture suitable to accompany food.

To blend — is to thoroughly mix herbs and spices to create an appealing flavour, eg. mixed herbs and bouquet garni, some mustards.

There are excellent brochures available from herb and spice companies explaining how to use their products to enhance various types of food.

Herbs

Many of these herbs can be home grown and used either fresh or dried.

Basil
Camomile
Chervil
Chives
Dill weed
Fennel
French sorrel
Garlic
Garlic chives
Lovage
Lemon balm
Marjoram

Mint
Onion
Oregano
Parsley
Pennyroyal
Pineapple sage

Rosemary
Sage
Spearmint
Tarragon
Thyme
Winter savory

Spices

These spices are all available from commercial sources and may be purchased whole or ground.

Allspice
Anise
Bay leaves
Cardamom
Cloves
Coriander
Cumin

Ginger
Mace
Mustard
Nutmeg
Turmeric
Vanilla

Seeds (use sparingly)

Caraway
Celery
Mustard
Poppy
Sesame

Peppers and blends

Bouquet garni
Cayenne pepper
Chilli powder
Chinese five spice
Curry powder

Garam marsala
Paprika
Mixed herbs
Mixed spice
Mustard blends
Salad herbs

Sprouting seeds, legumes and grains

The sprouting of seeds, legumes and grains has grown in popularity in Western society in recent years. Sprouts are an important source of vitamins and minerals, and increase in nutritional value as they grow. They are also low in calories/kilojoules and are therefore excellent for those people intending to reduce their weight. Sprouting is also fun, economical and very rewarding.

Sprouts may be eaten at all stages according to the needs and tastes of the consumer. Seeds, legumes and grains are available from health food stores, but it is necessary to purchase seeds etc. that have been especially prepared for 'sprouting only'. Many seeds that are prepared for ground growth have been treated with chemicals and are definitely not suitable for sprouting; always ask before you buy.

Preparation and method

There are two types of containers which can be used:
1. The simplest method is to use a clean jar, cover the opening with gauze, muslin or stocking and secure with a rubber band.
2. There are round or square sprouting containers available from health food stores. They have two or three layers and enable you to grow several varieties at the same time.

Selection of seeds

Select the seeds of your choice and soak them overnight covered with tepid water. Next day, pour off the water and place the seeds onto a sprouter tray or in a jar. Cover the sprouts. Rinse the sprouts twice per day, or three times per day in hot or dry weather. Place them in a darkened cupboard or cover them with a darkened cloth; this will encourage the sprouts to germinate more quickly.

If using a glass jar, place it on a slight angle with the opening downwards to enable excess water to drain off. *Caution:* always drain sprouts well as excess water will become stagnant and the sprouts will smell and deteriorate.

Completed growing time and harvesting will vary with the different seeds, legumes and grains used. Test the sprouts as they grow.

Place the sprouts in sunlight just prior to harvesting so that they turn green in colour. I use sprouted grains just as the tiny white shoots are peeping through — again it depends on preference. See 'Tips on when to harvest sprouts' below.

Store the sprouts in the refrigerator in plastic bags and use them within two or three days of harvesting.

Seeds Alfalfa, sunflower.
Legumes Moong (Mung) beans, black beans, garbanzo (chick peas), fenugreek, lima beans, adzuki beans, soy beans, dried peas.
Grains brown rice, wheat, corn, millet, unpearled barley, rye, buckwheat.

Growing chart

Seeds/Grains	Dry measure	Approximate harvest time
Adzuki beans	½ cup	3–4 days
Alfalfa	2 tablespoons	3–4 days
Barley	½ cup	3 days
Brown rice	½ cup	4–5 days
Garbanzo (chick peas)	½ cup	3–4 days
Lentils	½ cup	3 days
Mixed seeds	½ cup	4–5 days
Moong (Mung) beans	½ cup	4–5 days
Rye	½ cup	3 days
Soy beans	½ cup	3–4 days
Wheat	½ cup	3 days

This guide is approximate and may be varied according to the amount of sprouts required.

Some legumes, for example, chick peas, soy beans and whole peas, may need soaking for up to 16 hours. After soaking mix thoroughly in lukewarm water and drain.

Suggested use of sprouts

Use sprouts in salads, stews, casseroles, 'fried' rice dishes, soup, sandwiches; mix with yoghurt and salad dressings, fruit drinks, vegetable drinks.

Serve rye, wheat or barley sprouts with your breakfast cereal.

Moong (Mung) beans are delicious eaten raw when they are only 2 days old. They are crunchy and taste very much like peas.

Brown rice is soft, crunchy and tasty when eaten just as the tiny white shoots are peeping through.

Grain sprouts improve the flavour of bread dough. Add 1 cup of ground sprouts to the dough mixture, and omit ½ cup each of flour and water. There will be some recipes using grain sprouts in different sections of this book.

Tips on when to harvest sprouts

Adzuki beans may be used in soups from Day 2 when the tiny shoots are just peeping through. Use them according to preference after Day 2 of sprouting.

Alfalfa seeds are at their best when harvested around the fourth day. Store in the refrigerator in a plastic container (covered). Use in several days or they will wilt.

Barley is very difficult to sprout. You need lots of patience. Use in salads and sprouted breads.

Brown rice takes a little longer to sprout. The tiny white shoots appear about Day 3. Eat them raw or cooked at all stages after Day 3. They taste a little like coconut, with that same chewy consistency. Use in scones, soups, salads, casserole dishes. The grain becomes soft and crunchy as the shoots appear.

Fenugreek is easy to sprout. It tastes a little like mustard and will enhance sandwiches and salads.

Garbanzo (chick peas) must be soaked longer than most other sprouts. They also take longer to sprout. They are used in soups, salads and oriental dishes.

Moong (Mung) beans are very versatile. They are easy to sprout and can be used from Day 2 of sprouting and harvested up to Day 5. They are sweet tasting, very much like watermelon. Use them raw or cooked in soups, salads and oriental dishes.

Wheat is a very easy grain to sprout. Harvest the sprouts according to requirements from Day 2 onwards. They are very sweet and suitable for use raw in salads or as a garnish on salads or cereals. Use cooked in soups, casseroles breads (see recipe, page 108).

Nuts and seeds

Chestnuts are the only nuts permitted on both the Regression and Maintenance Diets. All other nuts are *forbidden* due to their high fat/oil content. This includes almonds, walnuts, peanuts, pecans, hazelnuts, brazil nuts and cashews.

Chestnuts

There is no limit to the amount of chestnuts that may be eaten. They are available fresh from fruit and vegetable shops in the autumn. They are also available canned, either water-packed, whole or sliced, and in purée form (buy the variety with no added sugar).

To dry-roast chestnuts

Make a slit with a sharp knife in each side of the shell. Place the nuts onto a tray and bake them at 240°C in the oven for about 15 minutes and cool.

Shell and skin the nuts when cool and boil in water 20 minutes. Cool and chop them finely or use as you wish.

Baked shelled and skinned chestnuts may be dry-roasted in a moderate oven, then chopped and stored dry to use in cakes etc.

Use the canned water-packed chestnuts in a variety of vegetable dishes. They are very popular in Chinese dishes.

Use the canned purée in desserts, cakes and stuffings. Make sure you purchase the variety without sugar or additives.

Seeds

Sesame, poppy (maw), celery, mustard and caraway seeds may be used *sparingly only* due to their high fat/oil content. All other seeds, including pumpkin and sunflower seeds are not permitted. Use the seeds permitted as you would use a herb or a spice, in very small quantities, to flavour or decorate a dish.

Home drying

Over the past few years, the home drying (dehydration) of foods has become very popular. It is very economical to be able to dry fruit and vegetables when they are fresh, plentiful and cheap and then store them for use when they are out of season and more expensive. Dehydration also has the advantage of retaining the nutritional value of food and enhancing its flavour, and of course home dried food is free of sulphur chemicals and additives.

Home drying is very easy and food can be stored for several months if the preparation and storage instructions are carefully followed. Excellent books containing simple instructions are generally available with the purchase of your home drying machine.

Try to obtain organically grown foods to dry. There are a number of groups in different areas who are offering organically grown fruit and vegetables. If there is no such group in your area, then start your own.

Once you have a good supply of dried raw fruit and vegetables on hand (you can also dry your own herbs, following the instructions for different varieties), you will find that it has many uses. Your own favourite recipes can be adapted to include dehydrated foods. You can also use them uncooked as toppings and garnishes for salads, soups and casseroles, or for packed lunches and picnics.

Parents concerned that their children acquire good dietary habits will find that dried carrot rings, banana chips and fruit 'leathers' are an excellent in between snack. Children love to eat them and so will any guests who drop in.

I have dried:

celery stalks
mushroom slices
onion rings
potato slices
tomato slices
zucchini slices
apple slices

banana chips
orange rings (including the peel)
lemon rings (including the peel)
pineapple rings (serve with pre-
    dinner drinks or dips)
strawberries

Note: Dried vegetables are always acceptable on the Pritikin diet, but remember to stay within the guidelines when eating dehydrated fruit.

Exercise

The World Health Organisation defines fitness as the ability to carry out daily tasks with vigour and alertness, without undue fatigue and with ample reserve to enjoy leisure pursuits and meet unforeseen emergencies.

It is not surprising that people who are on the high complex carbohydrate, high fibre eating programme are better equipped to handle stress, more socially aware and more at peace. They are more vigorous physically, with greater endurance; this has been demonstrated in recent athletic competitions. Aerobic exercise is a wonderful tonic for lifting depression.

Exercise is important for pregnant women who should consult their obstetricians for advice in selecting an appropriate exercise programme.

Warning

It is important to note that it is extremely dangerous to attempt vigorous exercise if you have been on the Western diet. One should not attempt any vigorous activity without having a cholesterol count, and its readings should be close to the accepted Pritikin readings. Please see a doctor who is familiar with the programme and have a medical check-up, particularly if you are over 35 years old. You may also require a stress test.

Aerobic exercise

This is exercise during which the body requires extra oxygen to produce the extra energy that is being used, for example, in walking, swimming and jogging. Aerobic exercise will make the heart beat faster and this will not only improve heart function but will aid the circulatory system.

In order for aerobic exercise to be effective it should be performed each day or at least three times per week and the heart beat should be maintained at approximately 75 per cent of your maximum rate for around 20 minutes.

Your pulse rate is calculated by subtracting your age from 220. 75 per cent of that figure is known as your training pulse rate. However, you should not let your activity raise your pulse rate above 130. If it does rise above this rate then slow down for a while and then speed up again.

Explanation of training pulse

If you are 50 years old, your maximum pulse rate would be 220 minus 50 = 170. 75 per cent of 170 is 127·5 which equals your training pulse.

To maintain your training pulse rate for around 20 minutes is your first goal and may take several weeks or even months to achieve. If you have a watch with a second hand then you can monitor your own pulse as you are doing your exercise.

Avoid violent and unaccustomed exercise and don't exercise when you are sick or tired. Do not make yourself puff and be unable to talk at the finish of your exercise.

Walking will be the easiest exercise to perform, particularly if no exercise programme has been undertaken for some years. Walking can induce a weight loss when combined with this eating programme. Commence walking gradually at a casual pace, just over 3 kilometres per hour. When your body is coping with this pace, increase the pace gradually until you are walking at 5 to 6 kilometres per hour. Walk faster as your endurance grows. This will increase the efficiency of your heart and circulatory system, make you breathe deeper, your heart beat faster and every part of your body benefit as the muscles and tissues are flushed with oxygen from the blood stream.

Points to remember

- Do not attempt any vigorous exercise unless you are on a high complex carbohydrate, high fibre, *low fat* and *cholesterol* eating programme.
- Always have a warm up and a cool down period.
- Dress according to the weather but have a warm pullover in case it does get cold.
- Dress casually and comfortably, and wear jogging shoes or runners. Wear track suit or shorts.
- To calculate your pace, a pedometer is of great assistance. Distance is divided by time = rate.
- Do not jog unless your doctor allows it—jogging is quite dangerous when the body has not been used to an exercise programme.
- If you are over 35 years old have a medical check-up first.

Remember: No matter how light or heavy the exercise cholesterol will *not* burn. Any excess is retained in the body, particularly the arteries where it does the most harm.

When you start the programme

Tips to help keep you on the programme

- Make up a batch of Pritikin wholemeal scones (either sweet or plain) and keep them in the cupboard. They will keep for several days and be a blessing when you are hungry. Recipes are in the 'Bread, Scones and Pastries' section of this book and *It's Only Natural*.

- Cook up a large serving of brown rice to have in the refrigerator — this can be made up quickly into 'fried rice' or creamed rice, used in salads or eaten plain.
- Cook up casseroles made from vegetables of choice and have them on hand to eat during the day — re-heat when you are hungry.
- Eat a banana or unwaxed apple.
- Bake plenty of potatoes in their jackets for the family to eat. *Note:* potatoes are *not* fattening, but should not be eaten if you have arthritis.
- Make up and refrigerate Pritikin approved sandwich fillings. Make a sandwich with approved Pritikin bread or make toast from the bread and spread it with approved Pritikin spreads (see recipes in *It's Only Natural* or in this book).
- Approved Pritikin bread is now available in most health food stores and supermarkets making it now much easier to have toast, sandwiches etc. If you wish you can make your own bread (see recipes in 'Breads, Scones and Pastries' section).
- Have a jar of croutons made from the approved Pritikin bread recipe to flavour casseroles, salads and casseroles. Have a jar of bread crumbs made from approved Pritikin bread recipe to use as a topping on casseroles etc.
- Prepare salad vegetables of choice, for example, carrot rings, celery, radishes, corn kernels, and put into plastic bags to take out with you to nibble on trips. Make carrot and corn 'sandwiches' by placing corn between carrot slices — tastes great and is nice and crunchy.
- Use herbs and spices, lemon juice and vinegar to flavour recipes especially when you first start this programme and are eliminating your salt intake. They will add flavour to your food in the absence of salt whilst your taste buds are becoming accustomed to the new flavours.
- Make up a bowl of oatmeal to eat when you are hungry. Sprinkle it with cinnamon and add skim milk liquid.
- If you are in a hurry and very hungry make up a pikelet recipe (see recipe in 'Bread, Scones and Pastries' section of this book). Mix it with a mashed banana or grated carrot or apple, and add a dash of cinnamon or nutmeg and you have an acceptable dish. Pikelets are great to make for afternoon teas etc.
- Grow your own sprouts and have these on hand to add to soups, salads, casseroles and sandwich fillings. Learn to eat them on their own — they are quite filling. See section 'Seeds, Legumes and Grains'.
- Make up new Pritikin recipes and introduce them to the family gradually. Try to have approved Pritikin cakes on hand — there are plenty of recipes available.

Cheating

I do not encourage people to cheat. If you are a relatively fit person, and occasionally feel the need to cheat, then by all means do so, however be very strict with yourself in the days that follow to make sure that you make up for it by strictly adhering to the programme.

If you are a person who has a serious illness or disorder then it is not in your best interest to cheat — even the smallest of indiscretions could well have disastrous results and it is certainly not worth the risk.

I always think that the only person you harm when you cheat is yourself.

Tips to help when you are dining out

The opening of more restaurants across Australia has made it much easier for people to eat out and have Pritikin food. However, if you are living in an area where you do not have the advantage of a Pritikin restaurant then this is my advice on how to eat out and eat Pritikin.

If you know well in advance that you are going to be dining out then telephone the restaurant and explain carefully to the chef that you are on the Pritikin programme for health reasons.

Maintenance diet

- Do not eat your meat allowance for the day until you go out to dinner. Ask the chef to steam a small piece of the leanest fish on the menu without salt, fat, oil or any additives except perhaps a lemon wedge. You will by now know the size of the portion you are allowed.
- Ask the chef to steam you some vegetables without salt, sugar, fat or oil to be served with the fish.
- Order a side salad without dressing, oil, salt etc. You may like to order this as your entrée.
- Order fresh fruit for dessert.
- Ask for water over ice as a beverage.
- Take along some approved Pritikin bread with you.

Regression diet

As above, except for the meat allowance, when you should use your *weekly* meat allowance and order a lean steamed portion of fish as above.

Note: If you are a working person, make up some of the suggested foods from these tips to help you get started on the programme and have adequate supplies of food on hand.

Preparation of food

The ease of preparing food will be of great help when you change to this new way of eating. It will be necessary to rid yourself of your old habits and adopt some new and easier ones. As you know, the food is to be minimally processed and may be eaten *raw* or *cooked*, or a combination of both according to the climate and your taste preferences.

Balancing your diet

In order to get all of the essential minerals, vitamins and roughage that the body requires, plus the correct amount of amino acids, it is recommended that you:
- Eat at least 2 kinds of grain foods per day.
- Eat 1 piece of citrus fruit per day.
- Eat 3 pieces of fruit per day.
- Eat raw vegetable salads every day.
- Eat some raw or cooked green or yellow vegetables every day.
- Eat potatoes (not if you have arthritis) every day.
- Ensure an adequate intake of vitamin B_{12} by eating a small quantity of meat per week.
- Eat sweet potatoes, green beans and peas once or twice per week.
- Add unprocessed bran to your food.
- Eat at least 6 to 8 small meals per day. This will curb your appetite and keep your blood sugar at a constant level (neither high or low).

To gain weight add more grain food to your diet and eat more meals per day.

To lose weight reduce the amount of grains with your meals and eat more vegetables.

Hints when preparing food

- Always have a soup to start a meal.
- Use plenty of garlic, herbs and spices, lemon and vinegar to add flavour to a meal.
- Steam vegetables to retain their flavour, vitamins, minerals and nourishment.
- Eat a large mixed salad, particularly lettuce and either raw or cooked vegetables, with a meal.
- Use meat allowances as a flavouring, for example, in pizza, spaghetti, rice and pasta dishes.
- Do not use fat or oil for cooking, but use a non-stick pan and use water, juice (unsweetened) or stock (defatted) for sauté.
- When sweetening is required use bananas, dates, grated apple, natural sultanas or fresh or canned (sugar free) fruit.

- Use bread that has no fat/oil, salt, sugar or preservatives added. Get your local baker to make some up for you, make your own, or buy the approved Pritikin bread.
- Do not eat refined white flour products at any time. Always use stone-ground plain or self raising flour.

Helpful hints when preparing meat

- Use lean meat, trim off all fat and either grill, steam or bake it in the oven. Pot roasting is also acceptable. To 'pot roast' steam meat in a little water and then gently brown the outside when the water has evaporated.
- Always wrap and dry meat with a paper towel to soak up any fat.
- Always remove the skin of poultry, because it contains the most fat.
- Steam or bake fresh fish (low fat varieties) in a non-stick pan, dry with paper towelling and serve with freshly ground pepper and lemon or vinegar.
- *Never* barbecue meat. If you are at a barbecue then cook your meat on top of the barbecue in aluminium foil.
- Also see helpful hints in *It's Only Natural* by Suzanne Porter.

It is not necessary to buy many extra cooking utensils, but it would be advisable to invest in a blender if possible and a non-stick frying pan is essential (inexpensive to buy in supermarkets and variety stores).

Suggestions for required equipment

Non-stick frying pan and cake tins, taking care to use them according to the instructions and warnings. It is not permissible to use any type of grease, oil or fat film on the inside of cake tins, dishes or pans before cooking any recipe. Even 'lightly' greasing the tin will add extra fat to your intake. Use aluminium foil to line insides of cake tins or trays or invest in non-stick ones.

Strainers
Grater
Wooden and plastic spoons
Tongs
Potato masher
Lettuce crisper
Glass or stainless steel basins for storage in refrigerator
Stainless steel or plastic bowls for freezer storage
Stainless steel or enamel saucepans
Glass and stainless steel mixing bowls
Paper towelling
Aluminium foil
Steamer
Plastic slides for use with non-stick pan
Seed sprouter or glass jar and muslin
Blender (electric)

Vegetable crisper
Food processor (this implement is invaluable)

As you continue on this programme you will find that your taste appreciation level will alter and you will really begin to appreciate the subtle flavours of the food. You may never have known these flavours before because they were disguised with fat, salt and sugar. It takes a little time for you to appreciate these flavours but the rewards of feeling so well and full of energy will be so great that you will wonder why you didn't adopt this new way of eating sooner.

You will learn to:

Cook without fat and oil
Cook without sugar
Eat unprocessed bran
Use less meat
Find suitable food in supermarkets
   and health food stores
Dry roast vegetables
Do without coffee and tea
Buy more vegetables
Discard egg yolks
Make cakes, desserts, puddings,
   without fat, oil and sugar

Using the recipes

Ingredients
You may find some of the ingredients in this book hard to obtain. However, there are now specialist shops where they should be available.

Abbreviations
cm   centimetre
g   gram
kg   kilogram
MD   Maintenance Diet
RD   Regression Diet
mg   milligram
ml   millilitre

Oven temperatures	C	F	Gas Mark
Very slow	120°	250°	¼–1
Slow	140°	300°	2
Moderate	190°	375°	5–6
Hot	210°	400°	7
Very hot	230°	450°	8
Extremely hot	240°	500°	10

Comparative liquid measures

Metric	Imperial
1¼ ml	¼ teaspoon
2½ ml	½ teaspoon
5 ml	1 teaspoon
20 ml	1 tablespoon
65 ml	2 fluid ounces (¼ cup)
125 ml	4 fluid ounces (½ cup)
250 ml	8 fluid ounces (1 cup)
625 ml	1 pint (20 fluid ounces)

Comparative solid measures

Avoirdupois	Metric
1 ounce	30 g
4 ounces	125 g
8 ounces	250 g
12 ounces	375 g
16 ounces	500 g
24 ounces	750 g
32 ounces	1000 g (1 kg)

Soups

Making stock

Vegetable stock

Use vegetable tops and washed peelings and any 'old' vegetables that have become limp. Put them all into a quantity of water, cover and cook for several hours. Top up whenever necessary with extra water. Cool, strain and store.

Vegetable stock may be used straight away, placed in the refrigerator for several days or frozen for longer storage.

Save all left-over liquid from cooking for soup bases.

Chicken stock

Make as for beef stock. You can also use the remaining carcass of a cooked chicken. Boil it up in water, remove all bones and skin, and store in refrigerator or freeze as for beef stock.

Beef stock

Use fresh or left over lean red meat, cover with water and boil gently for 1 to 2 hours. Remove meat, allow to cool in refrigerator and gently 'lift off' the congealed fat from the surface.

Strain through several thicknesses of muslin to ensure catching any remaining fat. (If you don't have muslin use two coffee filters, one inside the other.)

Stock may be frozen and the fat then 'run off' the top with boiling water before use.

Fish stock

Use same method as for beef and chicken stock.

MD
Goulash soup

100 g lean round beef (fat and skin removed), cut into strips
1 large onion, sliced
4 cups stock (defatted)
4 cups water
2 tablespoons dry white wine
1½ cups tomato purée (no salt, no sugar)
1 bay leaf
1 tablespoon paprika
4 medium potatoes, peeled, cut into quarters
Pinch cayenne pepper
Caraway seeds (optional)
Fresh parsley, chopped
1 tablespoon cornflour, water to mix

Saute meat and onions in a little stock and water in non-stick pan (lid on). Place in large saucepan with stock, wine, tomato purée, bay leaf, and paprika. Simmer for 2 hours. Add potatoes and cayenne pepper ¾ hour before serving. Add cornflour just prior to serving. Remove bay leaf. Sprinkle with caraway seeds and parsley, and serve.

Serves 6–8.

Variation

MD
Goulash soup and dumplings

As for Goulash Soup but omit potatoes and add 12 tiny dumplings (see recipe in 'Bread, Scones and Pastries'). Turn dumplings over about 20 minutes before serving.

Variation

MD
Curried chicken and rice soup

As for Chicken and Rice Soup but add ½ to 1 teaspoon curry powder according to taste.

Beef and barley soup RD

¾ cup unpearled barley
½ cup split peas, mixed
½ cup broccoli flowerettes
1 medium onion, chopped
½ cup celery, chopped
8 cups beef stock (defatted)
¼ teaspoon garlic powder
1 tablespoon cornflour, extra water to mix
Pinch cayenne pepper (optional)

Place all ingredients into large saucepan, except cornflour and garlic powder. Gently simmer (lid off) until soup is thick and barley swollen. Add cornflour and garlic powder just prior to serving.
Serves 4–6.

Chicken and rice soup MD

2 chicken breasts cooked, chopped (skin and fat removed)
6 cups chicken stock (defatted)
1 medium onion, chopped
1 medium carrot, grated
1 large celery stalk, chopped
½ cup long grain wild rice
1 dessertspoon lemon juice
¼ teaspoon thyme
Dash cayenne pepper
2 tablespoons cornflour, extra water to mix

Sauté vegetables in a little chicken stock in a non-stick pan (lid on) until onion is tender (do not brown). Add vegetables with stock, rice, juice, thyme and cayenne pepper in large saucepan.

Gently simmer for 30–40 minutes until rice is cooked. Add chopped chicken about 10 minutes before serving. Thicken with cornflour.
Serves 4–6.

RD ## Tomato and cabbage soup

1 cup canned tomatoes, chopped (salt and sugar free)
1 medium onion, chopped
6 cups chicken stock (defatted)
1 stalk celery, chopped
¼ cabbage, shredded

1 green pepper, chopped (optional)
1 cup wholemeal pasta (eggless)
½ teaspoon oregano
Dash cayenne pepper
2 tablespoons parsley, chopped

Sauté onion in 2 tablespoons chicken stock in non-stick pan (lid off) until soft. Add celery and cabbage. Stir gently until mixed. Pour into medium saucepan with remaining ingredients, except pasta and spices. Gently simmer about 15 minutes, then add remaining ingredients and simmer a further 30 to 40 minutes. Add parsley and serve.
Serves 4–6.

RD ## Potato and tomato soup

2 medium potatoes, peeled and sliced
4 medium tomatoes, peeled and sliced
1 large onion, chopped
1 clove of garlic, crushed
4 cups chicken stock (defatted)
1 tablespoon tomato paste (salt free)
1 teaspoon grated lemon peel

2 tablespoons chives, chopped
1 bay leaf

Garnish — *small dollop of non-fat yoghurt (sugar free)* or *low fat ricotta cheese (1 per cent fat maximum) processed with a little skim milk*

Sauté onion and garlic in a little stock in non-stick pan (lid on) until soft. Do not brown. Place with potatoes, tomatoes, tomato paste, stock, peel, chives and bay leaf in large saucepan (lid on). Bring to the boil and gently simmer until potato is cooked, about 30 minutes.

Remove bay leaf. Purée soup in blender. Return to saucepan, heat through. Serve hot.
Serves 4.

Leek soup

RD

1 bunch (3) leeks, slice the white part and about ¼ green part only
1 medium onion diced
1 clove garlic sliced
6 cups vegetable stock or water
1 tablespoon dry white wine (optional)
4 tablespoons skim milk powder with extra water to mix
1 tablespoon cornflour with extra water to mix

Place leeks, onion, garlic and stock into large saucepan with the lid on and gently simmer for 30 minutes until vegetables are soft.
   Process in blender to chunky smooth consistency. Return to saucepan, add wine and mixed skim milk and cornflour about 10 minutes before serving.
   Serves 4-6.

This is a very subtle-flavoured soup, a most enjoyable dish and one I recommend. You may of course add various herbs and spices to alter the flavour, but try it as per recipe and see if you enjoy it.

Variation RD
As for Leek Soup but add 1-2 tablespoons of curry powder 15 minutes before serving *or* add more garlic to give a stronger garlic flavour according to taste.

Minestrone soup

RD

¾ cup red kidney beans
1 large onion, chopped
1 clove garlic, crushed
1 carrot, diced
1½ cups tomatoes, fresh peeled or canned, no added salt or sugar
1½ cups cabbage, shredded
1 cup fresh beans, chopped, tops and tails off
10 cups beef stock, defatted
¼ cup tomato paste, no added salt
¾ cup wholemeal spaghetti pieces
Dash cayenne pepper
Very small quantity grated sapsago or *geska* cheese, 1 per cent fat maximum
Fresh crusty Pritikin approved bread

Place all ingredients except cabbage into large saucepan (lid off) and simmer about 2 hours. Add cabbage 20 minutes before serving.
   Serve hot, topped with sapsago cheese, with crusty bread.
   Serves 6-8 people.

RD **Variation**
As for Minestrone Soup but omit red kidney beans and use ¾ cup lentils *or* ¾ cup Continental Bean Mix.

RD ## Green bean soup

4 medium potatoes, peeled and
   sliced thinly
1 small onion, chopped finely
1 clove garlic, crushed
8 cups chicken stock (defatted)
1 bay leaf

2 cups green beans, finely sliced and
   steamed
2 tablespoons skim milk powder
1 tablespoon cornflour with extra
   water to mix
Pinch cayenne pepper (optional)

Place potatoes, onions, garlic, stock and bay leaf in large saucepan (lid on). Simmer about ½ hour until potatoes are soft. Add cooked beans about 15 minutes before thickening with cornflour and skim milk powder mixed together. Remove bay leaf and serve.
   Serves 6–8.

RD ## Split pea soup

⅓ cup yellow split peas
⅓ cup green split peas
8 cups water or stock (defatted)
1 medium carrot, grated
1 medium onion, chopped

1 stalk celery, diced
Pinch garlic powder
Pinch paprika
2 tablespoons soy sauce (low salt)
Pinch cayenne pepper (optional)

Place all ingredients in large saucepan (lid off), except spices and soy sauce. Bring to boil, gently simmer for about 1½ hours. Add spices and soy sauce 10 minutes before serving.
   Serves 4–6.

RD ## Rich vegetable soup

1 medium onion, coarsely chopped
1 medium swede, chopped or grated
1 small turnip, chopped or grated
1 medium tomato, skinned, sliced
2 small carrots, chopped
1 small stalk celery with leaves,
   chopped
1 small apple, chopped

6 cups stock (defatted) or water
½ cup apple juice, unsweetened
½ tablespoon dried dill
¼ cup chopped parsley with extra
   for garnish
1½ teaspoons paprika
Dash cayenne pepper

Prepare and place all ingredients into large saucepan except herbs and spices. Bring to boil and gently simmer (lid off) about 1½ to 2 hours. Add herbs and spices about 20 minutes before serving.
   Garnish with chopped parsley.
   Serves 4–6.

Left-over soup   RD

6 cups stock (defatted) or water
1 tablespoon unpearled barley
1 tablespoon brown rice
1 tablespoon split peas
¼ cup mixed beans including chick peas plus all left-over cooked and raw vegetables or other suitable left-overs

Place all ingredients in large saucepan (lid off) and gently simmer 2 hours until thick.
Serves 4–6.

Variations:

Cream of left-over soup   RD
As for Left-Over Soup but add ¼ cup skim milk powder and 1 tablespoon cornflour in water 10 minutes before serving.

Curried left-over soup   RD
As for Left-Over Soup but add 1–2 teaspoons curry powder 15 minutes before serving.

Tomato-flavoured left-over soup   RD
As for Left-Over Soup but add ¼ cup tomato paste (salt and sugar free) and add ¼ cup dry white wine *or* add 2 tablespoons soy sauce (low salt).

Cream of prawn soup   MD

4 king prawns cooked, shelled, deveined, or ¼ cup cooked shrimp
1 medium onion, finely chopped
4 cups fish stock (defatted)
1 bay leaf
⅓ cup canned evaporated skim milk
1 pinch of garlic
1 pinch of ginger
1 pinch of marjoram
1 tablespoon of any white wine (optional)
4 tablespoons cornflour with extra water to mix
chopped parsley to garnish (optional)

Place all ingredients except canned evaporated skim milk, spices, wine and cornflour into medium saucepan. Gently simmer until onion is soft, about ¾ hour.

Add milk, spices, and wine 10 minutes before serving. Thicken with cornflour. Remove bay leaf before serving.

Garnish with chopped parsley.
Serves 4.

Variations   MD

Add 1–2 tablespoons tomato paste (salt free). Stir into soup prior to serving.

Add 1 clove or more crushed garlic to taste *or* add 1–2 teaspoons curry powder.

MD ## Cream of lobster soup

As for Cream of Prawn Soup but add ½ cup cooked lobster.

MD ## Cream of oyster soup

As for Cream of Prawn Soup but omit prawns and add 8 chopped fresh oysters.

MD ## Cream of chicken soup

As for Cream of Prawn Soup but omit prawns and add 1 cup chopped steamed chicken pieces (fat and skin removed).

MD ## Fish chowder

200 g lean white fish (bones, skin removed)
6 cups fish stock (defatted)
3 medium sized potatoes, diced
1 small onion, diced
1 medium carrot, grated
1 stalk celery, diced
⅓ cup dry white wine (optional)
Pinch cayenne pepper
¼ cup skim milk powder with extra water to mix
1 tablespoon cornflour with extra water to mix
parsley for garnish

Place all ingredients in large saucepan (lid on) except skim milk and cornflour. Gently simmer 1 hour until soup is fairly thick. Add mixed skim milk and cornflour just prior to serving.
Serves 4–6.

MD **Variation**

Add 2 teaspoons curry powder 15 minutes before serving, *or* add 1 tablespoon tomato paste (salt free) 15 minutes before serving.

MD ## Scallop soup

8 scallops cleaned, washed and drained
4 cups fish or chicken stock (defatted)
3 medium potatoes, peeled and chopped
1 onion, chopped
¼ cup canned evaporated skim milk
2 tablespoons cornflour with extra water to mix
1 shake garlic powder
Dried parsley

Place all ingredients in large saucepan except milk, cornflour and herbs. Keep lid off. Gently simmer for about 1 hour until potatoes are soft. Add milk, cornflour, and herbs.
Serves 4.

Salads

Apple and carrot salad   RD

2 medium sized yellow apples, cut into slices lengthwise
2 cups carrot, grated
1 cup watercress
2 tablespoons alfalfa sprouts
½ cup special French dressing (see recipe in 'Dips, Dressings and Sauces')
1 teaspoon poppy seeds (optional)
1 dish lined with lettuce leaves

Arrange watercress around edge of dish. Fill the centre with grated carrot. Arrange sliced apple around watercress and on top of grated carrot. Top with alfalfa sprouts and sprinkle with poppy seeds. Gently pour over dressing.

Serves 4–6.

RD ## Beetroot and apple salad

2 medium sized beetroot, cooked, peeled and diced
1 cup green skinned apple, diced
1 cup red skinned apple, diced
¼ cup chives, chopped
½ cup non-fat yoghurt, sugar free
¼ cup vinegar
¼ cup fresh orange juice

Mix together beetroot, apples and chives.
    Thoroughly mix the liquids and gently fold through beetroot mixture.
Serves 4–6.

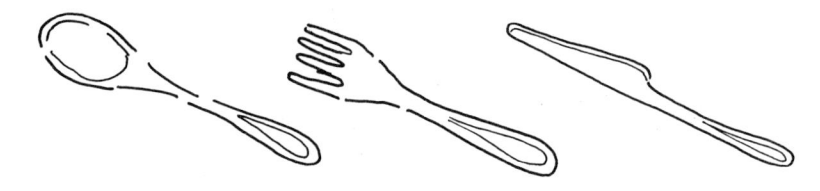

RD ## Endive salad

2 cups curly endive lettuce, torn into pieces
1 cup mung bean sprouts, matured
¼ cup green pepper, seeded and diced
¼ cup button mushrooms, sliced
½ cup water chestnuts, sliced
¼ cup soy sauce dressing (see recipe in 'Dips, Dressings and Sauces')
¼ cup garlic or onion flavoured croutons to garnish (see recipe in 'Breads, Scones and Pastries')

Gently toss all the ingredients with the soy sauce dressing. Garnish with croutons.
Serves 4–6.

RD ## Beetroot and pineapple salad

2 medium sized beetroot, cooked, peeled and diced
2 cups fresh or unsweetened pineapple pieces
1 tablespoon mint, chopped (optional)
½ cup non-fat yoghurt, sugar free
¼ cup vinegar
¼ cup unsweetened apple juice

Mix together beetroot, pineapple and mint.
    Thoroughly mix the liquids and gently fold through the beetroot mixture. This is a very colourful salad as the beetroot colours all the ingredients. Don't be put off by the colour.
Serves 4–6.

Caraway slaw   MD

4 cups cabbage, shredded
1 onion, chopped
1 stalk celery, chopped
1 tablespoon caraway seeds
¼ cup currants, undipped

2 tablespoons lemon juice
½ cup non-fat yoghurt, sugar free
¼ cup unsweetened apple juice
1 pinch mustard powder

Combine cabbage, onion, celery, caraway seeds and currants in a glass dish.

Thoroughly mix remaining ingredients and fold into cabbage mixture. Chill in refrigerator.

Serves 4–6.

Corn and potato salad   RD

3 cups cooked potatoes, peeled, chopped into chunks
1 cup fresh corn kernels, steamed
¼ cup chives, chopped

About ½ to ¾ cup mayonnaise (see recipe in 'Dips, Dressings and Sauces')
sprig of parsley to garnish

Gently fold the potatoes, corn and chives with the mayonnaise. Chill in refrigerator before serving.

Serves 4.

Zucchini, new potato and adzuki bean salad   RD

2 small zucchini, sliced thinly
20 tiny new potatoes, boiled and peeled
½ cup adzuki bean shoots (3 days growth only)

¾ cup tarragon dressing (see recipe in 'Dips, Dressings and Sauces')

Gently mix zucchini, potatoes and adzuki beans. Toss thoroughly with tarragon dressing. Chill in refrigerator for 2 to 3 hours before serving.

Serves 4–6.

Cherry, grape and pineapple salad   RD

1 cup fresh or unsweetened dark pitted cherries
1 cup fresh or unsweetened pineapple pieces
1½ cups sultana grapes

½ cup diced celery
1 tablespoon chives, chopped (optional)
2 tablespoons fresh orange juice
4 lettuce cups

Gently toss all ingredients in orange juice and divide equally into the four lettuce cups. Chill and serve.

Serves 4.

RD ## Tomato salad

2 large tomatoes, thickly sliced　　*1 tablespoon vinegar*
¼ cup chives, chopped
2 tablespoons dried basil
2 tablespoons unsweetened apple juice

Arrange sliced tomatoes in a single layer around a serving platter. Sprinkle with chives and basil. Mix liquids together and spoon over tomatoes. Chill for at least 4 hours to allow herbs to flavour tomatoes. Serve chilled.
　Serves 4.

RD ## Island rice salad

1 medium sized red apple, diced
1 tablespoon lemon juice　　*Chopped mint or parsley and ¼ cup*
2 cups brown rice, cooked　　*fenugreek sprouts (2 to 3 days)*
1 stalk celery, diced　　*to garnish*
⅓ cup shallots, chopped
⅓ cup mayonnaise (see recipe in 'Dips, Dressings and Sauces')
1 tablespoon vinegar

Mix apple in lemon juice and combine with all the other ingredients except mayonnaise and vinegar.
　Combine mayonnaise and vinegar and toss with the other ingredients just before serving. Top with garnish.
　Serves 4–6.

RD ## Jellied beetroot

2 cups fresh beetroot, peeled and grated　　*1 teaspoon orange rind, grated*
1 tablespoon gelatine
3 tablespoons boiling water
1 cup water
¼ cup fresh orange juice

Place grated beetroot in a glass dish.
　Dissolve gelatine in boiling water. Add to water and orange juice and heat together in a saucepan until well mixed. Cool the liquid slightly and pour over beetroot, mixing well. Top with grated rind.
　Allow to cool, and refrigerate until set.
　Serves 4.

Cucumber special   RD

2 cups cucumber, peeled and sliced
1 small salad onion, chopped
Grated lemon rind of 1 lemon
2 tablespoons lemon juice
½ cup non-fat yoghurt, sugar free
2 tablespoons unsweetened apple juice
2 tablespoons canned evaporated skim milk, 1 per cent fat maximum
1 teaspoon chopped mint to garnish

Arrange cucumber slices and chopped onion in a dish. Thoroughly mix all other ingredients and gently fold through cucumber. Chill. Garnish with chopped mint.
Serves 4.

Mixed vegetable salad   RD

¼ cup corn kernels (fresh or cooked)
¼ cup peas, cooked
¼ cup green beans, chopped and steamed
¼ cup carrots, diced and steamed
2 cups potatoes, diced and steamed
¼ cup chives, chopped
¼ cup each red and green peppers, chopped
3 eggs hard boiled (yolks discarded), sliced (save 3 slices for garnish)
¼ cup adzuki bean sprouts (3-4 days growth)
¾ cup mayonnaise (see recipe in 'Dips, Dressings and Sauces')
1 tablespoon of Quick Tomato Sauce (see recipe in 'Dips, Dressings and Sauces')
Sprig of parsley to garnish

Bowl lined with cabbage leaves

Mix mayonnaise and tomato sauce. Combine all other ingredients, being careful to keep egg white slices intact. Fold in mayonnaise mixture and pour into lined bowl.
   Decorate with 3 egg white slices and parsley.
Serves 4-6.

Variations   MD

As for Mixed Vegetable Salad but add ½ cup steamed, diced, chicken or turkey pieces (defatted) *or* add ½ cup cooked lobster, chopped.

Variation
Sunshine island rice salad   MD

Add ⅓ cup currants, undipped, *or* ⅓ cup natural raisins, chopped, *or* ¼ cup dates, pitted and chopped.

RD ## Deluxe coleslaw

6 cups green cabbage, shredded
1 cup red cabbage, shredded
1 red apple, diced
¼ cup corn kernels, fresh
¼ cup peas, steamed
1 green pepper, seeded and diced
3 medium sized mandarins, peeled
  and segmented

2 shallots, chopped
½ cup non-fat yoghurt, sugar free
¼ cup canned evaporated skim
  milk, 1 per cent fat maximum
¼ cup cider vinegar

Combine all liquids. Mix together all other ingredients and gently fold in mixed liquid. Turn out into a cabbage lined bowl.
   Serves 8.

RD ## Oriental salad

2 cups mung bean sprouts,
  (4–5 days' growth)
1 carrot, grated
1 salad onion, finely chopped
1 cup fresh or unsweetened
  pineapple pieces
½ cup cooked asparagus, sliced
  across

1 tablespoon shallots, chopped
½ cup garbanzo (chick peas),
  cooked
¾ cup special French dressing
  (see recipe in 'Dips, Dressings and
  Sauces')
½ cup sprouted wheat (sprouted
  2–3 days only)

Place all ingredients in a glass dish and gently toss through with French dressing. Chill and serve.
   Serves 4–6.

Variations

MD As for Oriental Salad but add 1 cup diced, steamed chicken or turkey (skin and fat removed) *or* add ½ cup chopped prawns

RD ## Radish salad special

½ cup radishes, sliced
1 medium sized zucchini, sliced
  thinly
¼ cup fresh corn kernels
¼ cup shallots, chopped
2 cups lettuce, torn into small
  pieces

1 tablespoon fresh orange juice
1 tablespoon tarragon vinegar
1 tablespoon parsley, chopped
¼ teaspoon salad herbs

Combine the liquids and gently toss through the mixed vegetables and herbs. Chill in the refrigerator.
   Serves 4.

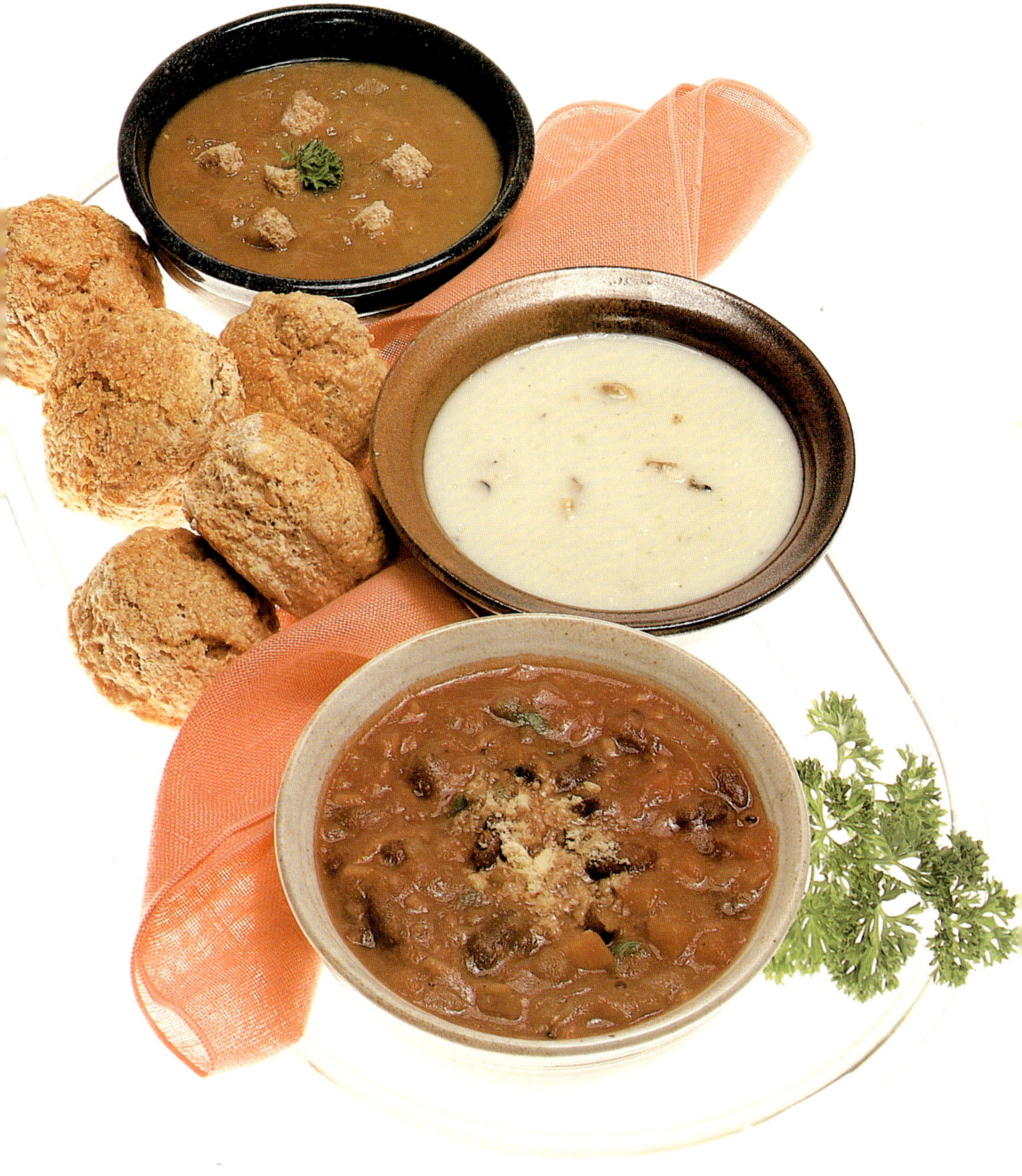

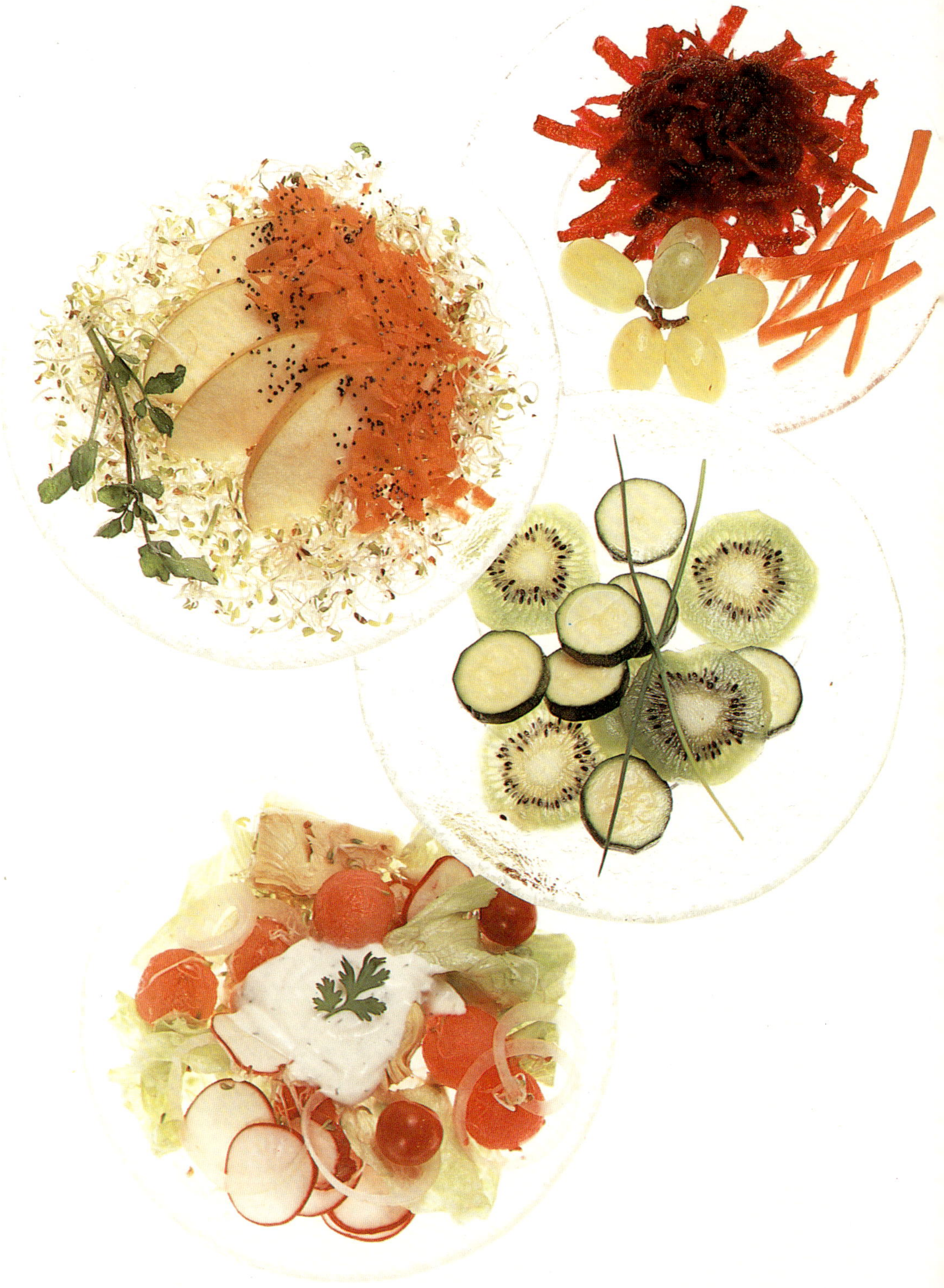

Salad toss supreme RD

½ medium sized lettuce, tear into pieces
½ cup alfalfa sprouts
2 artichoke hearts, cooked, cut into quarters
8 cherry tomatoes
1 small salad onion, cut into rings
2 radishes, cut into rings
1 cup watermelon balls
½ cup dill dressing (see recipe in 'Dips, Dressings and Sauces')
⅓ cup garlic croutons to garnish (see recipe in 'Bread, Scones and Pastries')

Gently toss all ingredients in dill dressing. Garnish with garlic croutons.
Serves 4.

Kiwi fruit salad RD

4 kiwi fruit, peeled and sliced
½ cup special French dressing. (see recipe in 'Dips, Dressings and Sauces')
2 small zucchini, sliced thinly

Gently coat Kiwi fruit and zucchini with the French dressing. Refrigerate for about 4 to 6 hours.
Serves 4.

Overleaf: Minestrone soup (RD), (page 41), Cream of Oyster soup (MD) (page 44), Split pea soup (RD) (page 42), with croutons (RD), Sprouted rice scones (RD) (page 108).

Opposite: Jellied beetroot (RD) (page 48) and Carrots Julienne (RD), Kiwi fruit salad (RD) (page 51), Apple and carrot salad (RD) (page 45), Salad toss supreme (RD) (page 51) with Dill dressing (RD) (page 120).

MD ## Waldorf salad

1 cup green apple, chopped in chunks
1 cup red apple, chopped in chunks
1 cup celery, sliced
¼ cup natural raisins, chopped
1 teaspoon lemon and orange peel (soak 1 hour in boiling water)
¼ teaspoon grated fresh ginger

1 teaspoon lemon juice
½ cup mayonnaise (see recipe in 'Dips, Dressings and Sauces')
4 lettuce cups
Mung bean sprouts (2 to 3 days growth only) to garnish

Toss together all ingredients except liquids.
 Mix lemon juice and mayonnaise and gently fold through apple mixture. Divide and serve in lettuce cups. Garnish with mung bean sprouts.
 Serves 4–6.

RD ## Wheat salad

2 cups wheat kernels, preferably organically grown
Enough tepid water to cover wheat
Juice of 1 lemon
½ cup mung bean sprouts (sprouted 2 days only)
1 tomato, seeds removed, and chopped

½ cup French dressing, (see recipe in 'Dips, Dressings and Sauces')
1 tablespoon fresh parsley, chopped

This recipe takes 2 days to make.
 Place wheat and tepid water in a saucepan, bring to the boil and immediately remove from heat. Allow to stand and cool in water. Add lemon juice. Pour into a glass bowl and stand for 36 to 48 hours.
 Drain the wheat—it should be nice and plump. Gently fold in mung bean sprouts, tomato, French dressing and parsley. Refrigerate.
 Serves 8–10.

Vegetables

Artichokes (globe) RD

1 artichoke per person
1 clove of garlic, crushed
2 tablespoons lemon juice
Enough water to cover artichokes

String to tie around the artichokes
to keep the leaves closed

Tie each artichoke with string. Slice the tops and stem off each artichoke leaving enough stem so that the leaves will not fall off.

Place the water in a saucepan, adding the garlic, lemon juice and artichokes. Bring to the boil and simmer, uncovered, for 30 to 40 minutes, until the leaves pull out and the bottom (stem end) is tender.

The artichoke leaves can be eaten hot or cold. The hearts can also be used in salads, etc.

RD   Asparagus mornay flan

1 can asparagus or 1 cup cooked asparagus
1 medium sized onion, chopped
1 medium sized carrot, diced
3 boiled egg whites, chopped, yolks discarded
1 tablespoon non-fat, uncreamed cottage cheese
1 tablespoon chives, chopped
2 cups thick White Sauce 2 (see recipe in 'Dips, Dressings and Sauces')
½ cup dry breadcrumbs, (see recipe in 'Bread, Scones and Pastries')
2 teaspoons sapsago cheese, grated, 1 per cent fat maximum
Plain pastry to cover 25 cm flan tin (see recipe in 'Bread, Scones and Pastries')

Preheat the oven to 200°C. Line 25 cm flan tin and cover with pastry.
Make up the white sauce. Sauté onions in dry non-stick pan (lid on) until browned and soft. Fold onion, asparagus, carrots, egg whites, cottage cheese and chives into the thick white sauce and pour into the pastry flan. Top with breadcrumbs and sapsago cheese.
Bake 20 minutes in the oven and brown the top under the griller just prior to serving.
Serves 4–6.

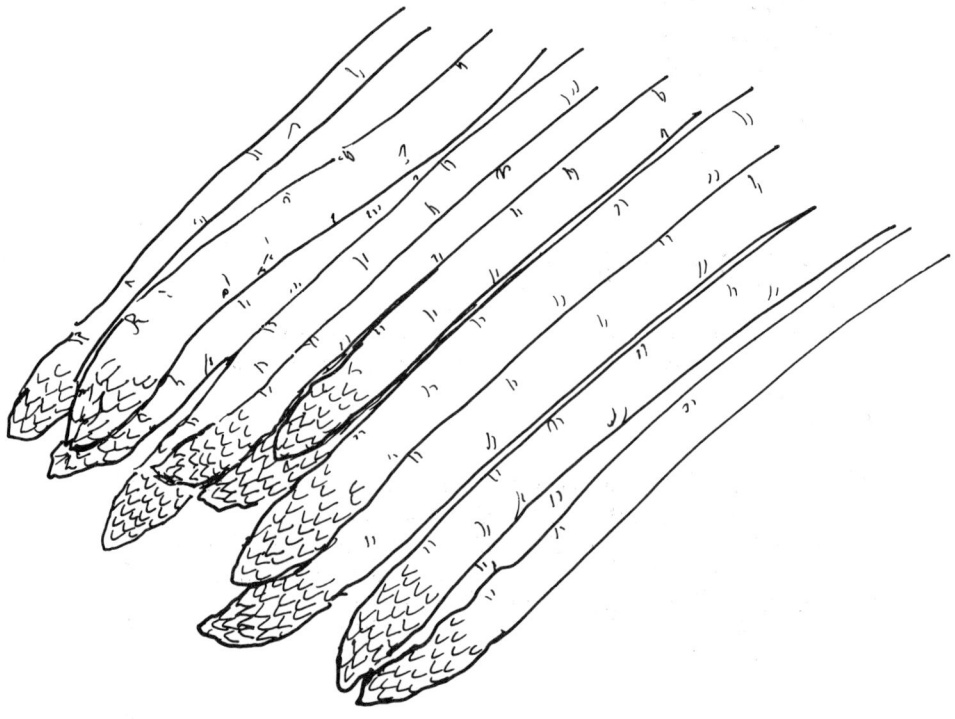

Candied sweet potatoes RD

4 cups sweet potatoes, peeled and sliced
½ cup water
½ cup unsweetened apple juice
Extra water

Mix the water and apple juice together in a non-stick pan. Arrange the sweet potato rings flat side down and separate. Gently brown each side, turning the slices over until all the liquid has evaporated. If the potatoes are not quite cooked add some of the extra water. Keep hot until serving.
Serves 4.

Au gratin potatoes RD

4 large potatoes, scrubbed, dried, thinly sliced
1 small onion, chopped
3 cups stock (defatted) or water
½ cup unsweetened apple juice
1 tablespoon tomato paste, salt free
1½ tablespoons arrowroot with extra water to mix
¼ teaspoon rubbed sage
Dash of paprika
½ teaspoon dried parsley

Preheat the oven to 200°C.
 Arrange the sliced potatoes. Top the potatoes with the onions. Mix all the other ingredients, except the paprika and parsley and pour over the potato mixture. Sprinkle top with paprika and parsley.
 Cover and bake for 1½ hours, or until potatoes are cooked.
Serves 4–6.

Broccoli and cauliflower mornay RD

2 cups fresh broccoli, chopped in chunks
2 cups fresh cauliflower, chopped in chunks
1 small onion, finely diced
½ cup liquid skim milk
1 tablespoon cornflour, extra water to mix
¼ cup dry breadcrumbs (see recipe in 'Bread, Scones and Pastries')
½ tablespoon grated sapsago or geska cheese (1 per cent fat maximum)
Paprika to sprinkle on top

Steam together broccoli, cauliflower and onion for 5 minutes only. Turn into a medium sized ovenproof dish.
 Heat milk with mixed cornflour until thickened. Stir well. Pour the mixture over the broccoli and cauliflower. Top with breadcrumbs, grated cheese and paprika.
 Place under the griller until top is golden brown.
Serves 4.

RD ## Brussels sprouts

20 tiny brussel sprouts
½ cup tomato paste, salt free
⅓ cup stock (defatted) or sprout water

⅛ teaspoon cayenne pepper
½ teaspoon sesame seeds (optional)

Trim the sprouts and cook them quickly for about 10 to 15 minutes. Drain the water, saving some of the water for stock. Return the sprouts to the saucepan. Keep warm.

Mix together the tomato paste, stock, cayenne pepper and seeds. Gently bring to the boil, and pour over the sprouts. Serve hot.

Serves 4–6.

RD ## Corn and carrot pudding

1½ cups corn off the cob
1 medium sized onion, chopped
1 medium sized carrot, grated
½ red pepper, seeded and chopped
½ green pepper, seeded and chopped
1 clove garlic, crushed
½ cup non-fat yoghurt, sugar free

⅓ cup skim milk liquid
2 egg whites, yolks discarded
3 tablespoons stoneground wholemeal self raising flour
½ tablespoon unsweetened apple juice concentrate
½ teaspoon dry mustard

Preheat the oven to 180°C.

Sauté corn, onion and grated carrot (dry with lid on) constantly turning to brown slightly. Fold in chopped peppers and garlic, gently simmer and cool.

Thoroughly blend remaining ingredients in a processor until smooth and fold into the cooled mixture. Pour into a medium sized square oven-proof dish (with lid) and bake in the oven 30 to 40 minutes.

Remove the lid 10 minutes before serving. Cut into serving size squares and serve hot with a salad or hot vegetables.

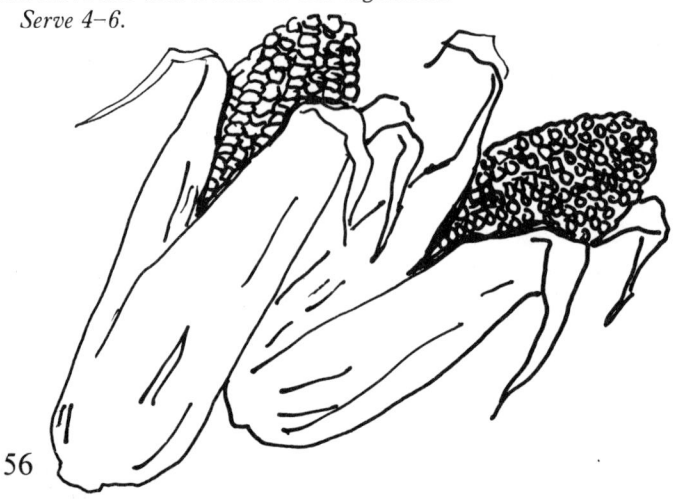

Serve 4–6.

Chunky island vegetable sauté RD

1 medium sized onion, chopped in chunks
1 carrot, cut into large slices
1 green pepper, seeded and cut into 6 strips
10 green beans, whole, ends removed
1 corn cob, sliced into rounds
1 medium sized zucchini, sliced in chunks
1 cup unsweetened apple juice
1 cup pineapple pieces, fresh

1 tablespoon tomato paste, salt free
1 tablespoon cornflour, extra water to mix
Pinch cayenne pepper
Pinch garlic powder
Pinch basil powder

Steam all the vegetables for 4 to 5 minutes only.
    Place apple juice, tomato paste, herbs and spices in a saucepan, bring to the boil and thicken with the mixed cornflour.
    Add the steamed vegetables and pineapple and gently coat with the liquid. Serve at once.
    Serves 4.

Scalloped potatoes RD

4 large potatoes, peeled, sliced thinly
1 tablespoon unsweetened apple juice concentrate

1 tablespoon soy sauce, low salt
2 cups water
1 tablespoon arrowroot, extra water to mix

Preheat the oven to 200°C.
    Arrange the potatoes in rows on a square ovenproof dish. Mix together all the remaining ingredients and gently pour over the arranged potatoes. Cover with a lid and bake in the oven for 30 minutes.
    Remove the lid and bake a further 30 minutes, until the potatoes are cooked. Serve hot.
    Serves 4–6.

Red cabbage sauté RD

4 cups red cabbage, shredded
½ cup unsweetened apple juice

1 tablespoon vinegar

Mix cabbage and juice in a non-stick pan and gently sauté, folding cabbage over as it cooks. Add the vinegar just before serving. Mix well. Serve hot.
    Serves 4.

RD

Mushroom soufflé pie

8 large open mushrooms, sliced
1 cup water
1 tablespoon dry white wine
1 tablespoon soy sauce, low salt
2 tablespoons canned evaporated skim milk (1 per cent fat maximum)
1 tablespoon non-fat, uncreamed cottage cheese
½ tablespoon unsweetened apple juice concentrate
½ teaspoon garlic granules
Pinch nutmeg
Pinch ginger
2½ tablespoons cornflour, mixed with water

Topping

2 egg whites, stiffly beaten (yolks discarded)
2 tablespoons canned evaporated skim milk (1 per cent fat maximum)
Pinch garlic powder

1 pastry-lined pie dish 25 cm round

Preheat the oven to 210°C.
 Gently simmer the mushrooms, water and wine in a saucepan for about 10 minutes. Thicken with the mixed cornflour, add the remaining ingredients. Cool and pour into the pastry lined dish.

Topping

Fold the milk and garlic into the stiffly beaten egg whites and spread evenly over the mushroom mixture.
 Place in the oven for about 20 to 30 minutes until the topping is golden brown and the pastry is cooked. Serve at once.
 Serves 4–6.

Snow peas Hawaiian style

RD

24 snow peas
1 cup fresh or unsweetened pineapple pieces
2 tablespoons unsweetened pineapple juice
1 pinch cinnamon

1 teaspoon grated orange peel

Top and tail snow peas and sauté peas and pineapple with the pineapple juice in a non-stick pan. Add the cinnamon and grated peel. Simmer about 2 to 4 minutes. Serve at once.
 Serves 4.

Creamed corn

RD

2 cups corn kernels, steamed
¾ cup white sauce (see recipe in
   'Dips, Dressings and Sauces')

¼ teaspoon sesame seeds
1 teaspoon dried parsley (optional)

Make up the white sauce. Mix the corn kernels and sesame seeds into the white sauce. Sprinkle dried parsley onto the top of each serving.
   Serves 4.

Spaghetti with vegie sauce

RD

1 medium sized carrot, grated
1 stalk celery, sliced
1 small onion, chopped
1 medium sized zucchini, sliced and
   cut into quarters
2 medium sized potatoes, diced
2 tablespoons Seasoned Flour 2,
   omitting curry (see recipe in
   'Dips, Dressings and Sauces')
1 cup water
¼ cup tomato paste, salt free

¼ teaspoon dried basil
¼ teaspoon oregano
1 bay leaf
1 cup water, extra
Quantity of wholemeal spaghetti,
   cooked and drained (hot) for 4
   servings

Make up the seasoned flour and toss all the vegetables in the plastic bag until well coated.
   Sauté the vegetables in a non-stick pan, tossing frequently to brown them, for about 5 to 10 minutes. Add 1 cup water, tomato paste, herbs and bay leaf. Gently simmer for a further 5 minutes and add remaining cup of water. Simmer another 5 minutes until potato is soft *not* mushy. Remove bay leaf. Serve hot on top of spaghetti.
   Serves 4.

RD Sunshine vegetable medley

8 tiny potatoes, unpeeled and scrubbed
12 snow peas, ends removed
1 parsnip, peeled, cut into quarters
8 yellow baby squash, halved across

Sauce

1 tablespoon soy sauce, low salt
1½ cups White Sauce 2 (see recipe in 'Dips, Dressings and Sauces')
¼ cup cauliflower flowerets, steamed
¼ cup broccoli flowerets, steamed

Preheat the oven to 180°C.
 Boil the potatoes until cooked, and drain. Steam snow peas, parsnip and yellow squash, and place in an ovenproof dish (medium size).
 Make up the white sauce and process it with the cauliflower and broccoli until smooth. Fold in the soy sauce. Pour over the vegetables and bake in the oven for 20 to 30 minutes.
 Serves 4.

RD Spiced vegetable medley

1½ cups Seasoned Sweet Sauce (see recipe in 'Dips, Dressings and Sauces')
1 teaspoon grated lemon rind
3 cups green beans, sliced, steamed
3 cups carrots, sliced, steamed

Steam beans and carrots together until cooked but still crisp. Pour the steamed vegetables into an ovenproof dish and keep warm.
 Make up the Seasoned Sweet Sauce and gently pour over the top of the vegetables, and sprinkle the grated lemon peel over the top. Serve at once.
 Serves 4–6.

RD Spiced parsnips

4 medium sized parsnips, peeled and quartered
4 tablespoons unsweetened apple juice
1 tablespoon soy sauce, low salt
1 teaspoon arrowroot, extra water to mix
¼ teaspoon allspice
¼ teaspoon cinnamon

Preheat the oven to 200°C.
 Steam parsnips for 8 to 10 minutes. Arrange parsnips in an ovenproof dish. Mix all other ingredients and pour over the parsnips. Bake 1 hour with the lid on. Parsnips should be well coated with the mixture.
 Serves 4.

Curried vegetable casserole   RD

2 medium sized carrots, sliced
2 potatoes, diced
¼ cauliflower, broken into flowerets
1 onion, chopped
1 cup corn kernels, fresh or canned
1 cup broccoli flowerets
6 brussel sprouts, peeled and halved
1½ cups water
1 bay leaf
2 tablespoons cornflour, extra water to mix
2 tablespoons canned evaporated skim milk, 1 per cent fat maximum
1½ teaspoons curry powder
¼ cup dry breadcrumbs (see recipe in 'Bread, Scones and Pastries')
1 teaspoon sesame seeds

Preheat the oven to 200°C.

Place all of the vegetables, water and bay leaf in a large saucepan and boil for 5 minutes (lid on). Thicken the mixture with the cornflour, add canned evaporated skim milk and curry powder.

Remove the bay leaf and pour the mixture into an ovenproof dish. Top with the breadcrumbs and sesame seeds and bake in an oven for 15 minutes.

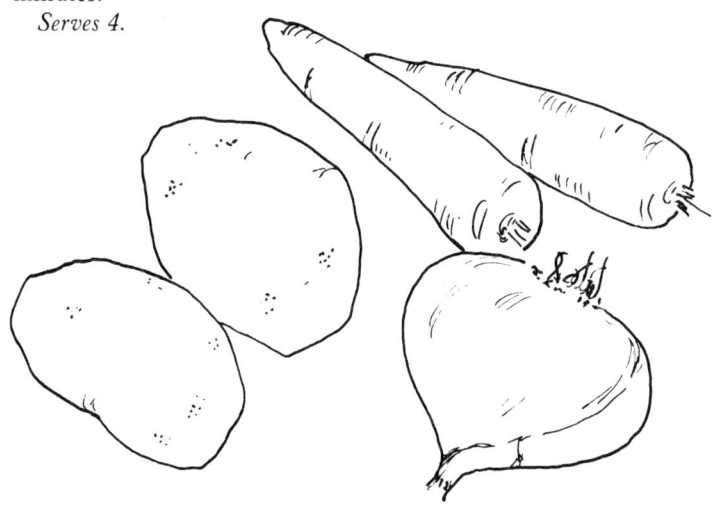

Serves 4.

Curried cabbage   RD

4 cups green cabbage, shredded
2 tablespoons unsweetened apple juice
1 tablespoon curry powder

Sauté the cabbage in a non-stick pan with the apple juice, folding the cabbage as it cooks for about 5 to 10 minutes.

Add the curry powder just before serving. Mix well. Serve at once.

Serves 4.

RD Fried rice special

2 cups brown rice, cooked, drained
1 small onion, chopped
1 medium sized carrot, grated
4 medium sized mushrooms, sliced
½ cup peas, cooked
½ cup corn kernels, raw
1 cup mung bean sprouts (2 days' growth only)
½ cup unsweetened apple juice
2 tablespoons soy sauce, low salt
1 tablespoon chives, chopped

Sauté the onion in a non-stick pan (lid on) in a little apple juice until soft. Add the remaining ingredients and gently fold until hot and thoroughly mixed, for about 4 to 5 minutes.
Serves 4.

RD Herbed chokos

4 medium sized chokos, peeled, seeded and cut into squares
¼ cup unsweetened apple juice
½ tablespoon cornflour, extra water to mix
¼ cup parsley, chopped
2 tablespoons chopped chives
1 tablespoon soy sauce, low salt
1 teaspoon dried thyme

Sauté chokos with the apple juice in a non-stick pan for about 10 minutes, or until tender.
   Mix the cornflour and all the other ingredients and gently pour over the chokos, tossing them to coat them well. Serve hot.
Serves 4.

RD Garbanzo sauté

1½ cups garbanzo (chick peas), soaked, cooked and drained
1 medium sized onion, chopped
1 medium sized carrot, sliced
1 cup water
½ cup fresh or unsweetened pineapple pieces
½ cup peas, steamed
½ cup unsweetened apple or pineapple juice
1½ tablespoons soy sauce, low salt
2 tablespoons Seasoned Flour 1, (see recipe in 'Dips, Dressings and Sauces')

Make up seasoned flour in plastic bag and toss in garbanzos, onions and carrots. Coat well. Turn out onto a non-stick pan and gently sauté (dry) tossing the ingredients for 2 to 3 minutes.
   Add the water, pineapple pieces and peas. Simmer a further 3 minutes continuing to toss the ingredients. Add the remaining ingredients and toss a further 2 to 3 minutes until well mixed. Serve at once.
Serves 4.

Cannelloni

4 large wholemeal pita breads halved (use top half only)
or 1 large mountain bread cut into quarters. (Mountain bread is a commercial bread very similar to wholemeal pita bread only about 2½ times larger than the large pita bread.)

Filling

4 cups silver beet steamed, chopped and drained
1 cup non-fat, uncreamed, cottage cheese

Sauce

1 medium sized onion, chopped
425 g (2 cups) tomatoes, peeled, no added salt
¼ cup water
1 tablespoon unsweetened apple juice concentrate
1 tablespoon arrowroot, extra water to mix
1 teaspoon basil
1 teaspoon oregano
¼ teaspoon rubbed sage
Pinch cayenne pepper

Preheat the oven to 200°C.
 Mix together silver beet and non-fat cheese, divide into four equal portions. Place a portion onto the edge of a pita top and roll it up. Trim the ends and place in a medium sized square ovenproof dish. Repeat for the remaining three pita breads.
 Sauté onion in water in a saucepan until soft (lid on). Add remaining ingredients except arrowroot and simmer for 5 minutes. Thicken with the mixed arrowroot and pour over the rolled cannelloni. Bake in the oven 15 to 20 minutes.
 Serves 4.

Hot vegetable combo

2 cups fresh green beans, topped and tailed, cut in half
1 cup fresh asparagus cuts
1½ cups fresh broccoli flowerets
1 red pepper, seeded, cut into strips
½ cup Seasoned Sweet Sauce 2 (See recipe in 'Dips, Dressings and Sauces')
¼ cup shallots, chopped

Steam together beans, asparagus, broccoli and red pepper for 5 to 10 minutes. Put aside and keep warm.
 Make the seasoned sauce and pour over the vegetables. Top with shallots and serve hot.
 Serves 4.

RD ## Sweet vegetable sauté

1 medium sized zucchini, sliced
2 medium sized carrots, sliced
1 onion, cut into rings
2 large open mushrooms, sliced
2 large potatoes, sliced
2 tablespoons Seasoned Four 1
(see recipe in 'Dips, Dressings
and Sauces')

1/4 cup unsweetened orange juice
1 1/2 cups water
1 tablespoon soy sauce, low salt

Preheat the oven to 210°C.
    Follow recipe for Seasoned Flour 1 and toss together all the vegetables and coat well with the mixture.
    Gently sauté the vegetables in a non-stick pan, tossing them constantly to brown about 5 to 10 minutes. Add the orange juice tossing the vegetables until the juice is absorbed. Add the water and soy sauce. Simmer for 5 minutes and turn out into an ovenproof dish (lid on) and bake in the oven about 1 hour. Remove the lid after 30 minutes.
    Serves 4.

RD ## Sweet 'n sour vegies

1 medium sized onion, sliced
1 stalk celery, chopped
1 clove garlic, crushed
1 cup button mushrooms, sliced
1/2 cup green beans, sliced finely
1 small zucchini, sliced in chunks
1 cup fresh or unsweetened
 pineapple pieces
1 small carrot, grated
1 tablespoon shallots, chopped
small quantity of water
1/2 small red pepper, seeded and
 chopped

1 1/2 cups prepared sweet 'n sour
sauce (see recipe in 'Dips,
Dressings and Sauces')

Sauté onions, celery and garlic in a non-stick pan (lid on) until onion soft. Add the remaining ingredients gently tossing for a further 3 to 4 minutes. Pour over the prepared sauce, simmer a further minute and serve at once.
    Serves 4.

Variation

RD ## Sweet 'n sour vegies and rice

As for Sweet 'n Sour Vegies but add 1 1/2 cups cooked brown rice, drained, just before serving.

Water chestnuts and beans RD

½ teaspoon grated fresh ginger
1 clove garlic, crushed
1 cup water chestnuts, sliced
½ cup corn kernels, fresh, steamed
2 cups cooked green beans, whole, steamed
⅓ cup chicken stock (defatted)

Sauté ginger and garlic in a non-stick pan (lid on) in a little of the stock for about 1 minute. Add water chestnuts, corn and remaining stock. Simmer a further minute.

Add the beans and simmer a further 5 minutes, stirring constantly to coat the vegetables. Serve hot.
Serves 4–6.

Swede and carrot special RD

4 cups carrot, diced
4 cups swede, diced
1 tablespoon canned evaporated skim milk
1 tablespoon soy sauce, low salt
⅛ teaspoon nutmeg

Steam together the carrot and swede, and mash them. Add the milk, soy sauce and nutmeg, stirring well to mix through the vegetables. Serve hot.
Serves 4–6.

RD ## Vegetable cheese pie

4 large ripe tomatoes, peeled and chopped
1 medium sized onion, chopped
1 cup open mushrooms, sliced
1 cup asparagus tips, cooked and drained
1 teaspoon dried basil
½ teaspoon oregano
¼ teaspoon rubbed sage
Pinch cayenne pepper

Sauce

1½ cups thick white sauce (see recipe in 'Dips, Dressings and Sauces')

½ cup non-fat, uncreamed cottage cheese
1 tablespoon unsweetened apple juice concentrate
Pinch cayenne pepper
1½ cups mashed potato at a fairly soft piping consistency

Garnish

¼ cup dry breadcrumbs, (see recipe in 'Bread, Scones and Pastries')
Sprig of parsley

Preheat the oven to 200°C.
Sauté together tomatoes, onion and mushrooms until onion is soft. Add asparagus and herbs gently, fold through the mixture and pour into a medium sized ovenproof dish. Set aside.
    Make the sauce and add cheese, apple juice and cayenne pepper. Pour over the cooked vegetables. Using a rose pipe gently pipe a border of potato around the edge of the mixture. Garnish with the breadcrumbs and bake in the oven about 15 minutes. Brown under the griller and garnish with sprig of parsley.
    Serves 4.

RD ## Tomato baked beans

1½ cups red kidney beans, cooked and drained

Sauce

1 tomato, peeled and chopped
1 small onion, chopped
2 tablespoons tomato paste, salt free
½ cup unsweetened apple juice

¼ teaspoon basil
¼ teaspoon oregano
½ teaspoon garlic granules
1 tablespoon cornflour, extra water to mix
1 tablespoon dried parsley, chopped, to garnish

To make the sauce, sauté the tomato and onion in a non-stick pan (lid on) with a little water until the onion is soft. Add the remaining ingredients except the cornflour and simmer about 10 to 15 minutes. Cool slightly and process in blender until smooth.
    Return the mixture to the saucepan and thicken with the mixed cornflour. Add the cooked kidney beans, heat through and serve on slices of toasted Pritikin approved bread. Sprinkle with parsley.
    Serves 4.

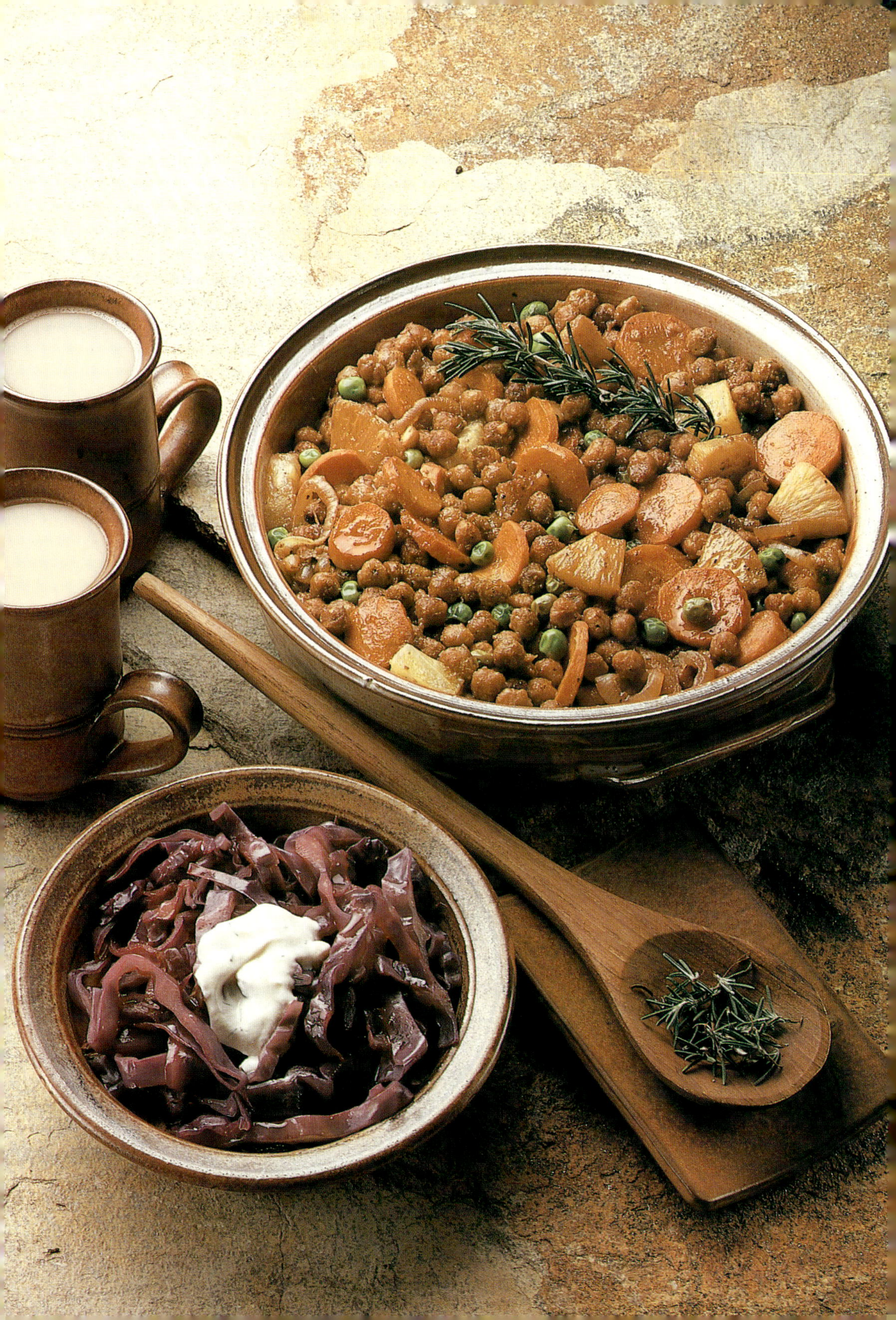

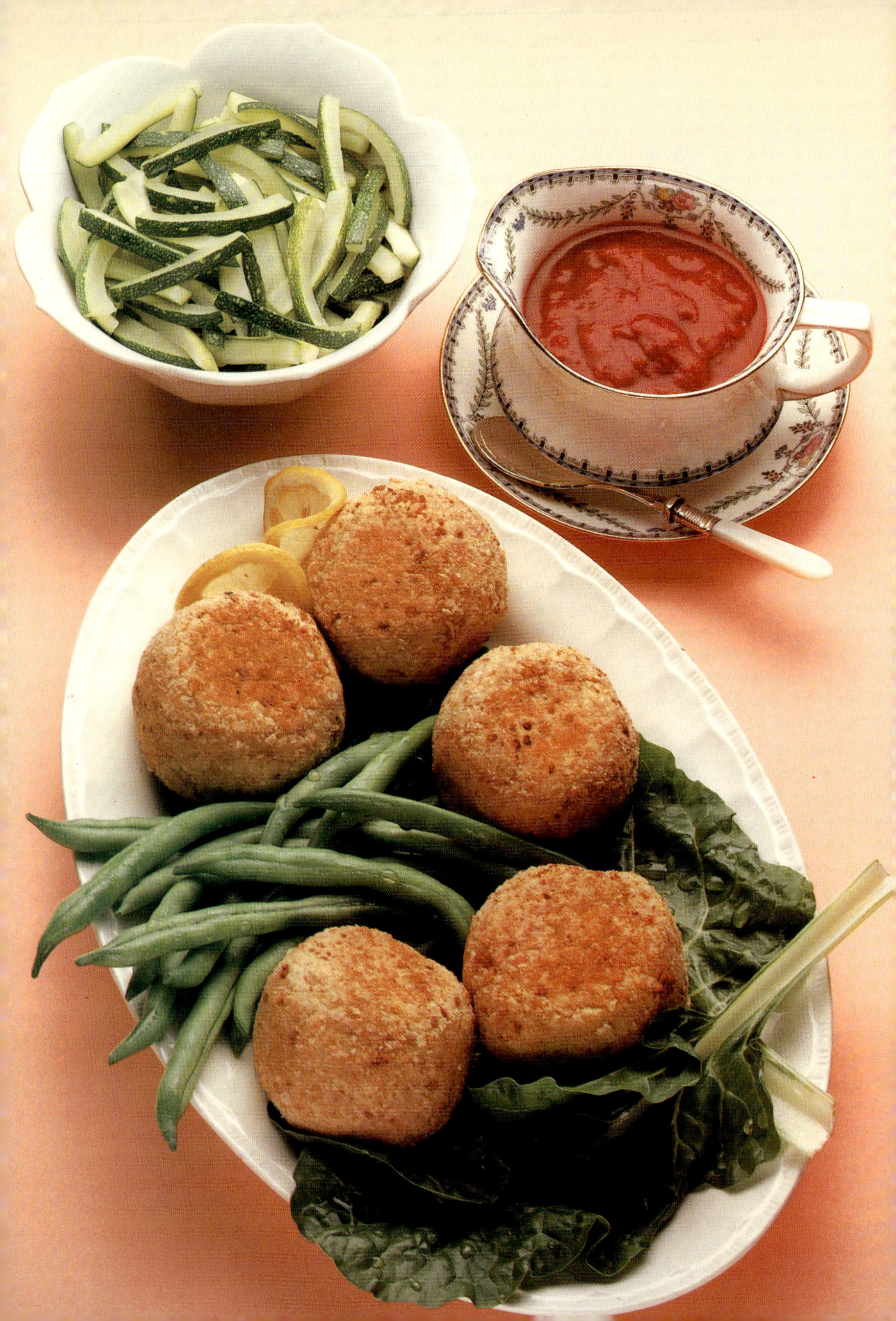

Tomato lentil special   RD

4 cups brown lentils
4 cups water
1 medium sized onion, chopped
1 carrot, sliced
1 stalk celery, sliced
4 cups tomato juice, salt free

½ green pepper, seeded, cut into strips
½ red pepper, seeded, cut into strips
¼ teaspoon basil
¼ teaspoon oregano
Pinch garlic powder

Put water, onion, lentils, carrot and celery in a saucepan and boil together for about 30 minutes. Add the tomato juice, pepper strips and herbs. Gently simmer a further 30 minutes and serve hot.
Serves 4.

Tomatoes hot spiced   RD

4 medium sized tomatoes, peeled (not stem end)
1 small onion, finely chopped
¼ cup unsweetened apple juice
¼ cup stock (defatted)

1½ tablespoons cider vinegar
¼ teaspoon ground ginger
⅛ teaspoon allspice
⅛ teaspoon cinnamon

Preheat the oven to 200°C.
Arrange tomatoes, stem end down, on an ovenproof dish.
Sauté onion in water in a non-stick pan (lid on). Add apple juice, cider vinegar and spices. Pour over the tomatoes and bake in the oven for 45 minutes. Baste the tomatoes with the sauce 2 or 3 times during cooking.
Serves 4.

Overleaf: Garbanzo sauté (RD) (page 62), Red cabbage sauté (RD) (page 57) topped with uncreamed cottage cheese (RD), approved herb tea and skim milk (RD).

Opposite: Curried salmon patties (MD) (page 80), Zucchini Julienne (RD), Plum sauce (MD) (page 105).

Meat, poultry and fish

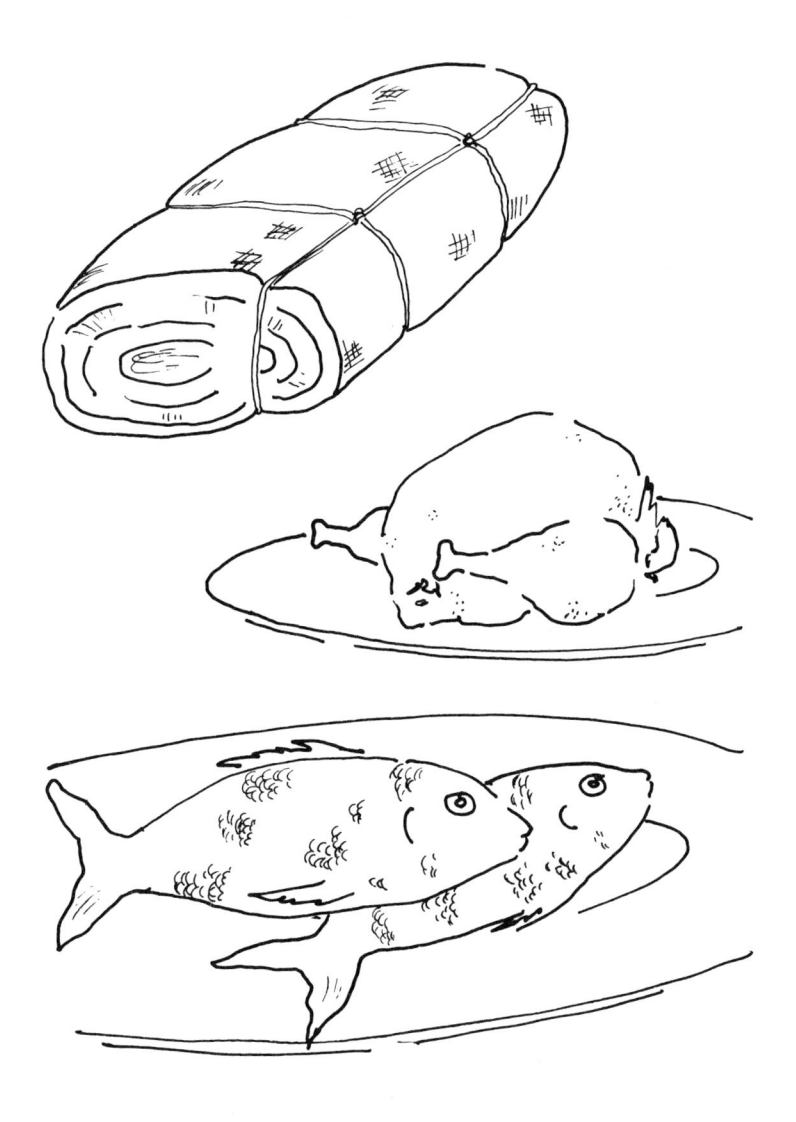

When selecting any meat, poultry or fish you should consult 'Meat, Poultry and Fish Choices' in the section 'Regression and Maintenance Diets — Permissible Foods' in this book.

MD ## Chinese 'stir fried' beef

400 g lean round beef, cut into strips 30 mm long, fat removed
1 clove garlic, crushed
¼ cup dry white wine
1 onion, sliced into rings
⅓ cup unsweetened apple juice
4 silver beet leaves and stalks, chopped
1 cup water chestnuts, sliced, drained
24 snow peas
1 can (425 g) baby corn
¼ cup beef stock (defatted)
2 tablespoons cornflour, extra water to mix
1 cup buckwheat noodles, cooked and drained

Marinate beef strips and crushed garlic in the wine. Sauté onion and apple juice in a non stick pan (lid on) until tender. Add chopped silver beet stalks, water chestnuts and snow peas. Simmer (lid on) for 2 minutes. Remove from pan and keep warm.

Sauté meat and wine at high temperature, turning the meat as it cooks, for 2 to 3 minutes. Add all the remaining ingredients, except the cornflour, gently tossing and mixing the ingredients at a high temperature.

Thicken with the mixed cornflour. Fold in the cooked noodles and serve at once.

Serves 4.

MD ## Curried ground beef

400 g lean round beef (ground), fat removed
3 medium sized onions, finely chopped
1 clove garlic, crushed
1¾ tablespoons curry powder
1 cup beef stock (defatted)
1 tablespoon unsweetened apple juice concentrate
2 tablespoons natural raisins
¾ cup peas, steamed
½ cup chestnuts, sliced, water packed
½ teaspoon powdered ginger
1 tablespoon cornflour, extra water to mix
4 cups cooked brown rice, hot
Chopped parsley and lemon slices to garnish

Sauté onions, garlic and curry in a little of the beef stock in a non-stick frying pan (lid on). Add the meat to the pan and gently fold into the onions. Brown lightly with lid off.

Add the remaining ingredients, except cornflour. Gently simmer for 15 to 20 minutes. Thicken with the mixed cornflour.

Serve hot over cooked rice. Garnish with parsley and lemon slices.

Serves 4.

Capsicum beef

MD

400 g lean round beef, sliced thinly, fat removed
1 cup marinade for meat (see recipe in 'Dips, Dressings and Sauces')
1 clove garlic, crushed
1 red capsicum, seeds removed, cut into strips
1 green capsicum, seeds removed, cut into strips
1½ tablespoons unsweetened apple juice
1 tablespoon soy sauce, low salt
½ teaspoon grated fresh ginger
1 tablespoon cornflour, extra water to mix
4 cups cooked brown rice, hot

Marinate the meat for 2 to 3 hours. After the beef has marinated, sauté it and the marinade in a non-stick pan. Add the remaining ingredients, except cornflour. Simmer for 1 hour (lid on) and thicken with cornflour mixed in a little water. Serve on top of cooked brown rice.
Serves 4.

MD ## Stuffed 'Virginia' roast

400 g Virginia roast, fat and skin removed, with a pocket cut in the middle

Stuffing

1 cup breadcrumbs, soft
3–4 button mushrooms, chopped
Good pinch sage

Good pinch garlic powder
1 small onion, chopped
½–1 tablespoon water to bind

or use stuffing of choice from It's Only Natural

Preheat the oven to 230°C.
    Mix together the stuffing ingredients and fill the meat pocket. Sew over the front of the pocket or tie string over the opening to prevent stuffing falling out. Place the meat in an oven cooking bag and put onto a wire cake rack in a roasting dish.
    Bake about 1 hour. Do not dry out the meat; always keep it in the oven cooking bag. Serve with roast potatoes, prepared in a non-stick frying pan (see recipe in *It's Only Natural*).
    Serves 4, 100 g each.

MD ## Lean beef olives

Six 48 g thin slices of lean round beef, fat removed

Stuffing

2 cups breadcrumbs (see recipe in 'Bread, Scones and Pastries')
½ teaspoon garlic granules
½ teaspoon rubbed sage

1 medium sized mushroom, finely chopped
½ cup vegetable stock or water
6 wooden tooth picks

Take each piece of meat and roll it into an oblong square (5 cm x 10 cm approximately). Mix all the ingredients for the stuffing and divide the mixture into six equal portions.
    Place a portion of stuffing onto the meat slice and roll it up into a roll. Secure the end with a tooth pick. Proceed with the remaining five slices of meat in the same manner.
    Place the six beef olives into a non-stick frying pan, cover with a lid and gently and slowly cook each olive, making sure to turn them to cook all sides. Leave the lid on the pan for about ½ hour. This will help cook the olives. Remove the lid for a further 15 minutes and brown on all sides. Remove the tooth picks before serving. Serve hot with your favourite vegetables.
    Serves 3, 2 per serve.

Beef stew with dumplings

MD

400 g lean round beef, cut into strips, fat removed
2 medium sized onions, diced
1 medium sized carrot, diced
½ cup dry white wine
1 tablespoon tomato paste (no added salt)
½ cup stock (defatted)
1 clove garlic, crushed
Pinch each of cayenne pepper, basil, oregano and rubbed sage
1 tablespoon cornflour, extra water to mix
8 small dumplings (see recipe in 'Bread, Scones and Pastries')

Sauté meat and onions with a little stock in a non-stick pan (lid on) for 5 minutes, turning to mix the meat. Add the remaining ingredients, except the cornflour, and simmer for another 10 minutes. Transfer the meat mixture into a medium saucepan and slowly simmer a further 45 minutes.

Add the dumplings 20 minutes before completion of cooking time. Be sure to turn the dumplings over to cook both sides. Thicken the meat mixture with the mixed cornflour before serving.

Serves 4, 2 dumplings each.

MD 'Seasoned' beef stew

400 g lean round beef, cut into fine strips, fat removed
1 onion, quartered and opened into segments
2 tablespoons Seasoned Flour 1, (see recipe in 'Dips, Dressings and Sauces')
1 cup water
½ cup unsweetened apple juice
1½ tablespoons soy sauce, low salt
1 cup fresh or unsweetened pineapple pieces
4 servings of cooked wholemeal noodles (egg free)

Put seasoned flour into a plastic bag, add the beef strips and shake the bag to coat the meat.

Sauté the onions and the seasoned beef in a non-stick pan with a little of the water. Constantly stir the onions and meat to avoid sticking and assist with browning, about 15 minutes.

Add water, apple juice and soy sauce to meat mixture, bring to the boil and transfer the meat mixture into a large saucepan (lid on) and simmer 1 hour. After 1 hour the mixture should be thick and the meat tender. Add the pineapple 10 minutes before serving. Serve over cooked wholemeal noodles.

Serves 4.

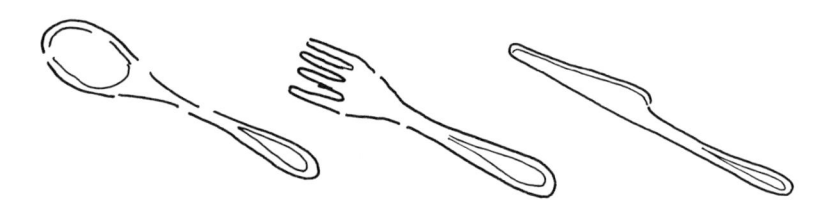

MD Lobster beef casserole

300 g lean round beef, sliced thinly, fat removed
100 g lobster, cooked and chopped
3 small onions, chopped
½ cup unsweetened apple juice
1¾ cup water
1 large potato, diced
¼ teaspoon garlic powder
1½ tablespoons cornflour, extra water to mix

Sauté onions and apple juice in a non-stick pan (lid on). Add the meat and cook at a high temperature for 2 minutes, stirring well. Reduce the heat and add the water, potatoes and garlic powder. Transfer the mixture to a saucepan and simmer (lid on) for a further 20 minutes or until the potato is soft. Add the chopped lobster and thicken with the mixed cornflour 10 minutes before serving.

Serves 4.

Spinach–beef casserole

MD

400 g lean round beef, cubed, fat removed
1 medium sized onion, sliced into rings
1½ cups cooked spinach
1 tablespoon soy sauce, low salt
1 tablespoon cornflour, extra water to mix

Marinade for beef

½ cup marinade (see recipe in 'Dips, Dressings and Sauces')

2 cups cooked brown rice, hot

Marinate cubed beef for 4 hours.

Sauté beef, marinade and onion rings in a non-stick pan (lid on) until meat is tender (about 15 minutes). Add spinach and simmer 4 to 5 minutes, mixing it well with the meat and onions. Gently simmer (lid on) for a further 30 minutes.

Add soy sauce and thicken with mixed cornflour 5 minutes before serving. Serve over a bed of hot brown rice.

Serves 4.

MD ## Chicken in soy sauce

Four 100 g chicken breasts, skin and fat removed
3 small carrots, cut into rings
½ cup water or stock (defatted)
½ cup dry white wine
¼ cup unsweetened apple juice
2 tablespoons soy sauce, low salt
2 tablespoon cornflour, extra water to mix

Seasoning
2 tablespoons stoneground wholemeal flour
½ teaspoon garlic powder
¼ teaspoon rubbed sage

Preheat the oven to 180°C.
   Place seasoning ingredients into a plastic bag and mix. Add the chicken breasts and thoroughly shake, coating well.
   Brown the chicken breasts both sides in a non-stick pan for about 15–20 minutes. Arrange them in an ovenproof dish.
   Mix wine and all the other ingredients and gently simmer in the pan. Thicken with the mixed cornflour. Pour over the chicken breasts, cover with the lid and bake in the oven about 30 to 40 minutes.

MD ## Chicken vegetable surprise

2 cups steamed chicken, chopped, skin and fat removed
1½ cups chicken stock, fat free
1 small onion, diced
¼ cup fresh corn kernels
¼ cup green beans, finely sliced
½ cup broccoli flowerets
1 stalk celery, diced
½ cup fresh asparagus, chopped, or other vegetable of choice
½ teaspoon garlic granules
½ teaspoon grated fresh ginger
½ tablespoon soy sauce, low salt
1 tablespoon arrowroot, extra water to mix
4 servings of cooked brown rice or cooked wholemeal noodles (egg free), hot

Steam all the vegetables 6 to 8 minutes. Drain and set aside hot.
   Mix all liquids, herbs and spices in a non-stick pan, heat through and add the mixed arrowroot and thicken. Add the vegetables and gently toss in the mixture. Add the chopped chicken last. Coat well with the sauce mixture. Simmer for 15 to 20 minutes.
   Serve hot with either cooked brown rice or cooked wholemeal noodles (egg free).
   Serves 4.

Chicken à l'orange   MD

Four 100 g chicken breasts, skin and fat removed
2 tablespoons Seasoned Flour 1 (see recipe in 'Dips, Dressings and Sauces')
Juice of 2 oranges
1 orange cut into rings, peel and pith removed
1 teaspoon orange rind
3 tablespoons water
2 cups cooked brown rice, hot

Coat the chicken with the seasoned flour and sauté in a non-stick pan with the water. Brown each side of the chicken. Cook about 20 minutes in all.

Pour the orange juice over the chicken and simmer a further 10 to 15 minutes. Add the orange rings and rind 5 minutes before serving. Serve hot over a bed of rice.

Serves 4.

Tomatoes with chicken   MD

Four 100 g chicken breasts, sliced, skin and fat removed
1 cup canned tomatoes, salt free
1 small onion, cut into rings
¼ cup dry white wine
1 tablespoon tomato paste
½ teaspoon garlic granules
¼ teaspoon basil
¼ teaspoon oregano
1 tablespoon cornflour, extra water to mix
Pinch cayenne pepper
¼ cup dry breadcrumbs (see recipe in 'Bread, Scones and Pastries')

Sauté onion in white wine in a non-stick pan (lid on) for 2 to 3 minutes. Add the chicken breasts and sauté with the onions for a further 10 minutes.

Add the remaining ingredients, except the cornflour, and gently simmer for 20 minutes (lid on). Thicken with the mixed cornflour before serving. Serve hot. Top each serving with a portion of the dry breadcrumbs.

Serves 4.

MD ## Curried chicken

400 g chicken breasts, skin and fat removed
3 small onions, sliced into rings
1 clove garlic, crushed
1 cup chicken stock, fat free
2 tomatoes, peeled and chopped
1 red pepper, seeded, cut into strips
1 cup green beans, sliced
¾ cup fresh or unsweetened pineapple pieces
1 tablespoon cornflour, extra water to mix
4 cups cooked brown rice, hot
½ cup unsweetened pineapple juice
¾ tablespoon curry powder

Chop the chicken into pieces. Sauté chicken in non-stick pan (lid on) with onions, garlic and a little chicken stock for 5 to 10 minutes. Add remaining ingredients, except cornflour. Gently simmer for about 20 minutes. Thicken with the mixed cornflour 5 minutes before serving. Serve over a bed of hot brown rice.
Serves 4.

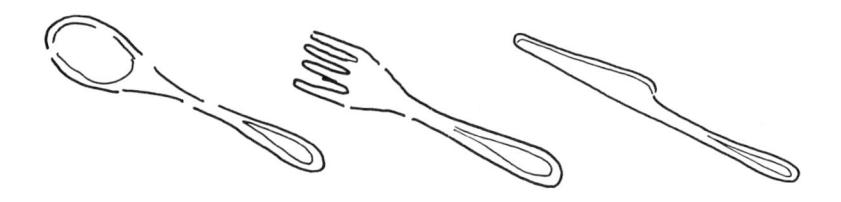

MD ## Creamed fish pan style

400 g lean white fish, cut into slices
1 small onion, cut into rounds
½ cup carrots, diced
½ cup cauliflowerets
¼ cup peas, steamed
¼ cup fresh corn kernels
½ cup mushrooms, sliced
2 cups white sauce made with fish stock (see recipe in 'Dips, Dressings and Sauces')
½ teaspoon dry mustard
1 teaspoon chopped parsley (optional)
2 tablespoons water

Sauté onions and all vegetables with the water in a non-stick frying pan about 2 to 5 minutes (lid on).
Add the fish slices, gently turning with the vegetables for a further 10 minutes. Pour the white sauce and herbs onto the vegetable mixture and simmer for a further 15 to 20 minutes (lid off) until fish is cooked. Serve hot.
Serves 4.

Baked fish asparagus MD

400 g lean white fish, cut into small squares
1 small onion, finely diced
1 stalk celery, sliced
1 tablespoon dry white wine
1 cup cooked asparagus, chopped
1 cup white sauce, made with defatted fish stock (see recipe in 'Dips, Dressings and Sauces')
⅛ teaspoon marjoram
Pinch nutmeg
Pinch garlic powder
¼ cup dry breadcrumbs (see recipe in 'Bread, Scones and Pastries')
1 tablespoon grated Sapsago cheese (optional)
1 cup cooked wholemeal macaroni (egg free)

Preheat the oven to 180°C.

Sauté the onion and celery in a non-stick pan with the white wine for 1 to 2 minutes. Add the fish squares and gently turn for about 2 minutes.

Gently fold all the remaining ingredients into the fish, except breadcrumbs and cheese. Simmer about 2 minutes and turn out into a medium sized ovenproof dish. Top with breadcrumbs and cheese.

Bake in the oven 15 minutes. Brown the top under the griller just before serving.

Serves 4.

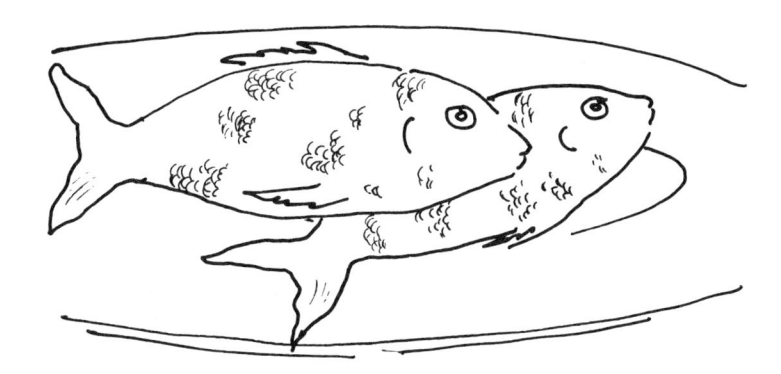

Baked fish casserole MD

400 g lean white fish, skin removed
1 cup button mushrooms, sliced
⅓ cup dry white wine
2 tablespoons shallots, chopped
1 tablespoon lemon juice
Grated rind of 1 lemon
⅛ teaspoon tarragon

Preheat the oven to 180°C.

Arrange the fish in a medium sized ovenproof dish. Mix all the other ingredients and pour over the fish. Cover and bake 45 minutes.

Serves 4.

MD ## Hawaiian fish

400 g lean white fish
1 cup fresh or unsweetened pine-
  apple pieces, drained
½ cup red and green pepper, seeded
  and diced
¼ cup shallots, chopped
⅓ cup celery, diced

4 tablespoons dry white wine
1 tablespoon lemon juice
1 tablespoon soy sauce, low salt
½ teaspoon ground ginger

Preheat the oven to 180°C.
Sauté peppers, shallots and celery with the wine in a non-stick pan for 3 to 4 minutes. Add the remaining ingredients, except the fish and pineapple. Simmer for 5 to 10 minutes. Arrange the fish in a medium sized ovenproof dish and pour the pineapple pieces over. Bake in the oven until fish is cooked.
Serves 4.

MD ## Curried salmon patties

220 g can of flaked salmon, skin
  and bones removed, rinsed under
  water
4 medium sized potatoes, cooked
  and dry mashed
1 small onion, diced
½–1 teaspoon curry powder
Pinch basil leaves

Pinch dry mustard
Pinch parsley flakes
Dash cayenne pepper (optional)
1 cup dry breadcrumbs (see recipe
  in 'Bread, Scones and Pastries')

Mix the salmon, potatoes, onion, curry and herbs together. Roll into round flat patties (about 6 or 8). Coat each in the breadcrumbs.
Brown on both sides in a non-stick frying pan. Serve with hot vegetables, or your favourite salad.
Makes 6 to 8.

Variation

MD ## Tuna patties

As for Curried Salmon Patties but omit salmon and curry powder and add 1 cup of drained tuna, skin and bones removed, rinsed under water.

MD ## Fish patties

As for Curried Salmon Patties but omit salmon and curry powder and add 1 cup steamed lean white fish, skin and bones removed.

Desserts

Vanilla custard   RD

2 cups water
¼ cup skim milk powder
1 tablespoon unsweetened apple juice concentrate
3 tablespoons cornflour, extra water to mix
1 teaspoon vanilla essence

Mix water, skim milk powder, apple juice and mixed cornflour in a saucepan. Slowly bring to the boil, stirring constantly to avoid lumps. Custard should be thick.
   Add vanilla essence just before removing from the heat.
   Serves 4, makes about 2½ cups.

RD ## Baked pears and rice

4 cups Creamed Rice Again
(see recipe in this section)
6–8 canned unsweetened pear halves
¼ teaspoon nutmeg, grated
1 cup cakecrumbs (use approved Pritikin cake to make crumbs)

Preheat the oven to 180°C.

Spread rice onto medium sized ovenproof dish. Arrange pears face down around the dish on top of the rice. Shake the grated nutmeg over the pears and sprinkle the cake crumbs on top. Bake in the oven for about 20 minutes.

Serves 4–6.

RD ## Banana custard

2 bananas, peeled and sliced
1½ cups water
2 tablespoons unsweetened apple juice concentrate
¼ cup skim milk powder
½ teaspoon vanilla essence
2 tablespoons cornflour, extra water to mix
Grated nutmeg (optional)

Thoroughly mix water, apple juice concentrate, skim milk powder, vanilla and cornflour mixed with water. Gently heat in a saucepan until 'custard' is thickened, stirring constantly so as not to develop lumps.

Set aside. When cool, add the sliced banana. Pour into a glass dish and sprinkle top with grated nutmeg.

Serves 4.

Variation

RD ## Brandy banana custard

As for Banana Custard but add 1 tablespoon of brandy when making the custard.

Opposite: Golden tart (RD) (page 90), Mixed fruit sauté (RD) (page 87).

Overleaf: Stuffed pears (RD) (page 89).

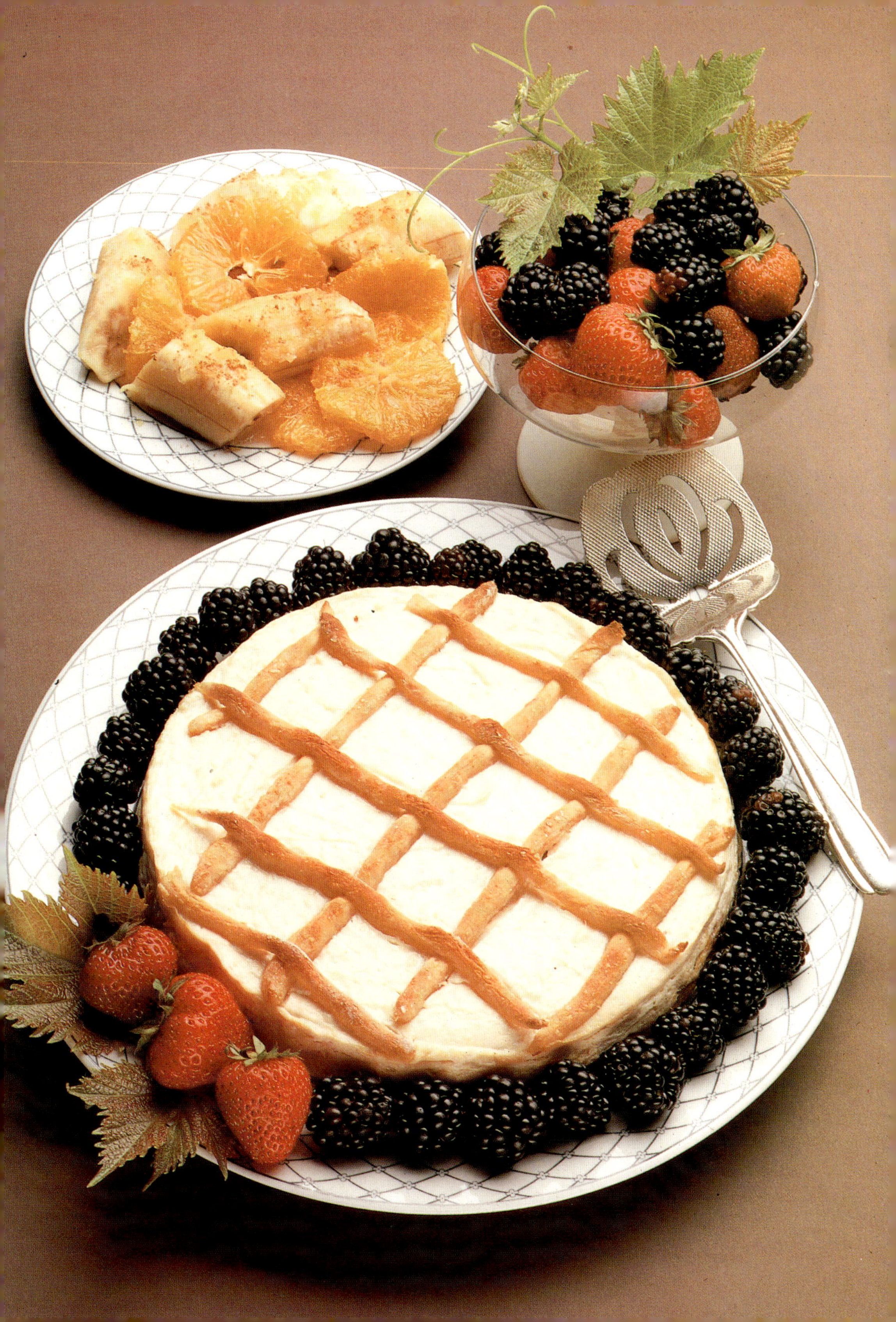

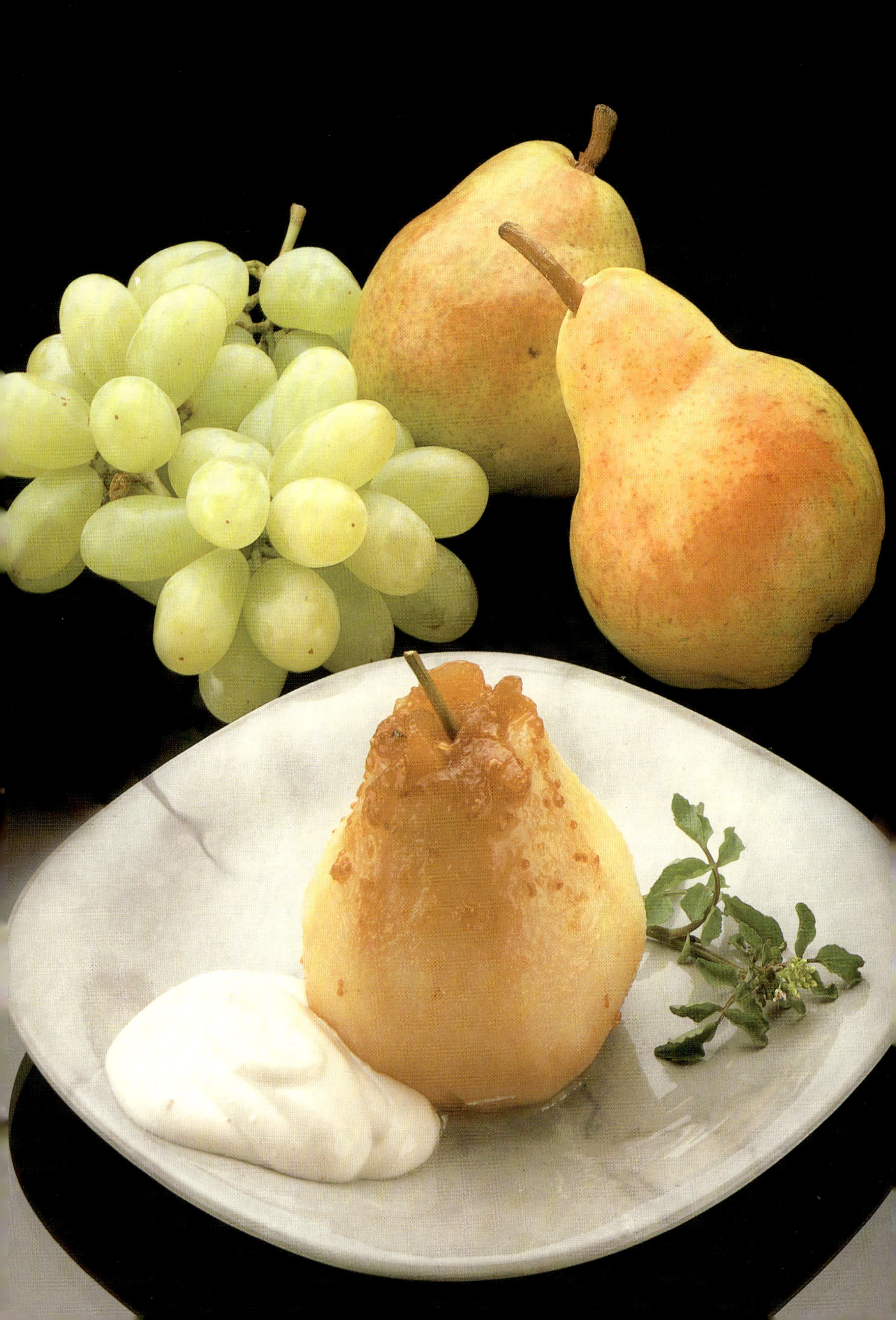

Vanilla 'ice-cream'   RD

Use this ice-cream sparingly. Refer to information about Dairy Foods in the section 'Regression and Maintenance Diets — Permissible Foods'.

1 can (375 ml) canned evaporated skim milk
2 teaspoons gelatine
2 tablespoons boiling water to mix gelatine
¼ cup skim milk powder
1 teaspoon vanilla essence
2 tablespoons unsweetened apple juice concentrate
2 egg whites, stiffly beaten, yolks discarded

Turn freezer to 'quick freeze'.

Place can of evaporated skim milk in freezer for about 2 hours. Remove can from freezer, open it up and beat the liquid until it becomes thick.

Dissolve the gelatine in the boiling water, add this to the mixture with the milk powder, vanilla essence and apple juice concentrate. Thoroughly beat the mixture, adding the stiffly beaten egg whites, until the mixture is thick and fluffy.

Place the mixture in a freezer tray or a plastic container and return to the freezer. Reduce the freezer temperature. Ice-cream will be set in about 1 to 1½ hours.

Variations

Carob-flavoured 'ice-cream'   RD

As for Vanilla Ice-cream but add 1 tablespoon of carob to the final beating.

Fruit 'ice-cream'   RD

As for Vanilla 'Ice-cream' but add ½ to 1 cup of your favourite unsweetened fruit to the final beating.

Creamed rice pudding   RD

2–3 cups Creamed Rice Again (see recipe)
2 bananas, peeled and sliced
Cinnamon (optional)
2 teaspoons unsweetened apple juice concentrate

Spread rice onto a medium sized ovenproof dish. Coat the bananas with the apple juice concentrate and arrange the coated bananas on top of the rice. Sprinkle the top with cinnamon.

Place under the griller until bananas are golden brown.
Serves 4.

RD # Creamed rice

1 cup brown rice
2½ cups water
¼ cup canned evaporated skim milk

Place rice and water into the top of a double boiler. Place some water in the bottom of the saucepan and bring the water to the boil. The heat will transfer to the top saucepan and will cook the rice. Keep the boiler steaming until the rice in the top is swollen and most of the water in the top is gone.

Add the canned evaporated skim milk about 10 minutes before rice is cooked.

Makes about 3 cups.

RD # Creamed sago

3 tablespoons sago
2¼ cups liquid skim milk
½ cup unsweetened apple juice
¼ cup canned evaporated skim milk
1 teaspoon vanilla essence
1 egg white, stiffly beaten, yolk discarded

Mix all ingredients in a saucepan, except the egg white. Over a low heat gently stir the mixture until the sago is thick and swollen. Be careful not to burn the mixture. Set aside and cool.

When completely cold, fold the beaten egg white into the sago mixture. Serve with unsweetened fruit of your choice.

Serves 3–4.

Fruited yoghurt RD

2 cups non-fat yoghurt, sugar free
2 tablespoons unsweetened apple juice concentrate
4 tablespoons canned evaporated skim milk or
4 tablespoons liquid skim milk

2 cups fresh or unsweetened stewed fruit of choice

Place all ingredients into a processor and process to chunky or smooth, as desired. Turn into a glass dish and refrigerate.
Serves 4.

Fruited jelly yoghurt RD

2 cups non-fat yoghurt, sugar free
3 tablespoons unsweetened apple juice concentrate
4 tablespoons liquid skim milk

1½ tablespoons gelatine
4 tablespoons boiling water to mix gelatine
2 cups fresh fruit of choice, mashed

Dissolve gelatine in the boiling water, set aside and cool.
Mix all other ingredients and thoroughly mix in the cooled gelatine. Turn the yoghurt mixture into a glass dish. Refrigerate until set.
Serves 4.

RD Pineapple upside-down cake

4–6 fresh or unsweetened pineapple rings
4–6 fresh or unsweetened pitted cherries or glacé cherries soaked for 1 hour in boiling water

Batter

½ cup fresh or unsweetened pineapple, processed
¼ unsweetened pineapple juice
¼ canned evaporated skim milk

Glaze

2 tablespoons unsweetened apple juice concentrate
2 tablespoons unsweetened apple juice

1½ cups stoneground wholemeal self raising flour
2 egg whites, stiffly beaten, yolks discarded

Preheat the oven to 180°C.

Glaze

Mix together apple concentrate and apple juice and spread onto the bottom of a small to medium sized ovenproof dish. Place the pineapple rings on top of the glaze and put a cherry in the centre of each ring.

Batter

Thoroughly mix all the batter ingredients, except the stiffly beaten egg whites. Fold in egg whites. Gently spread over the arranged pineapple rings.
  Bake for about 1 hour. Serve hot from the oven, topped with Vanilla Custard (see recipe this section) or More Exchange Cream (see recipe in 'Dips, Dressings and Sauces').
  Serves 4–6.

RD Pineapple 'fritters'

6 fresh or unsweetened pineapple rings
½ quantity of basic pikelets mixture (see recipe in 'Bread, Scones and Pastries')

1 cup Fruit Whip (see recipe in 'Dips, Dressings and Sauces')

Make the basic pikelets mixture into 6 pikelets. Set aside and keep warm.
  Brown each side of the pineapple rings in a non-stick pan and place on top of the warmed pikelets. Top each fritter with fruit whip. Serve immediately.
  Makes 6.

Mixed fruit sauté   RD

4 ripe bananas, cut in chunks
3 medium sized sweet oranges, peeled, sliced across
1 tablespoon ginger marmalade (see recipe in 'Spreads, Chutneys and Pastes')
¼ cup unsweetened apple juice
¼ teaspoon cinnamon

Thoroughly mix marmalade, apple juice and cinnamon together and heat through in a non-stick pan. Add the fruit and gently turn in the liquid until the fruit is well coated. Serve hot, topped with More Exchange Cream (see recipe in 'Dips, Dressings and Sauces').
   Serves 4–6.
Variation

Seasonal fruit sauté   RD

As for Mixed Fruit Sauté but use a combination of your favourite fruits or those that are in season.

RD ## Steamed 'spread' pudding

¼–½ cup of your favourite unsweetened fruit spread

Pudding

1 cup stoneground wholemeal self raising flour
1 tablespoon unsweetened apple juice concentrate
¼ tablespoon canned evaporated skim milk
1 egg white, yolk discarded
¼ cup skim milk liquid
Extra skim milk liquid

Pour the unsweetened fruit spread into the bottom of a 2-cup steamer.

Mix all the pudding ingredients together to make a cake batter. A little extra skim milk may be needed to bind.

When the pudding mixture is thoroughly mixed, gently pour on top of the fruit spread in the steamer. Cover well to keep out the moisture. Secure the lid in place.

Place the steamer in a large saucepan with enough water to steam the pudding. Steam about 1 hour.

Turn the pudding out onto a flat dish and allow the spread to run down the sides of the pudding. Serve hot, topped with Vanilla Custard (see recipe this section).

Serves 2.

RD ## Peaches 'n cream

1 large can unsweetened sliced peaches, drained
Grated rind 1 orange
⅛ teaspoon cinnamon
1 tablespoon stoneground wholemeal self raising flour
Nutmeg
3 peach slices for garnish

Topping

2 egg whites, stiffly beaten, yolks discarded
1 tablespoon skim milk powder

Preheat the oven to 220°C.

Arrange sliced peaches mixed with orange rind and cinnamon in an ovenproof dish.

Add flour and skim milk powder to the stiffly beaten egg whites. Spread the egg mixture over the peaches and shake grated nutmeg over. Bake in pre-heated oven for 30 minutes, until golden brown. Garnish with peach slices 5 minutes before end of cooking time.

Serves 4–6.

Stuffed pears
RD

4 medium sized ripe pears, peeled and cored
4 tablespoons Fig and Ginger Spread (see recipe 'Spreads, Chutneys and Pastes')
1 cup unsweetened apple juice
1 teaspoon lemon juice
2 teaspoons arrowroot, extra water to mix

Extra tablespoon Fig and Ginger Spread
Extra ½ cup unsweetened apple juice
1 tablespoon brandy (optional)

Preheat the oven to 180°C.

Place peeled and cored pears in medium sized ovenproof dish, standing upright. Place 1 tablespoon of Fig and Ginger Spread in the centre of each pear. Pour the cup of apple juice around the base of the pears and bake in the oven for 1 hour.

Meanwhile, mix the lemon juice, extra spread and apple juice together. Heat in a saucepan and thicken with mixed arrowroot. Stir constantly so as not to burn. Add brandy if desired. Spoon over baked pears and serve hot.

Serves 4.

Variation

Stuffed pears with apricot and pineapple
RD

As for Stuffed Pears but omit Fig and Ginger Spread and use Apricot and Pineapple Spread (see recipe in *It's Only Natural*).

Lemon sago jelly
RD

6 tablespoons sago
5½ cups water
½ cup lemon juice
Grated rind of 2 lemons

3 tablespoons unsweetened apple juice concentrate

Mix all the ingredients except apple juice concentrate in a saucepan and gently simmer until the sago has disappeared, about 10 minutes.

Add the apple juice concentrate and thoroughly mix. Cool and pour into glass dish and place in the refrigerator to set. Top with Exchange Cream of choice (see recipes in 'Dips, Dressings and Sauces').

Serves 4–6.

RD ## Orange jelly

1 cup fresh orange juice
¼ cup unsweetened apple juice
1 tablespoon gelatine (use sparingly according to Pritikin allowances)

2 tablespoons boiling water to dissolve gelatine
Grated rind of 1 orange

Dissolve gelatine in the boiling water, set aside.
  Place orange juice and apple juice into a saucepan and bring to the boil. Add the dissolved gelatine and mix thoroughly. Beat with a whisk. Add orange rind, pour into a dish and cool. Refrigerate to set.
  Makes 4 small servings.

Variation

RD ## Fruit jelly

As for Orange Jelly but add 1 cup of your favourite unsweetened fresh fruit, for example, bananas.

RD ## Golden tart

Citrus pastry to cover 20 cm cake tin (see recipe in 'Bread, Scones and Pastries')

Filling

1 cup ricotta cheese, non-fat or 1 per cent fat maximum
1 tablespoon lemon juice
1 tablespoon unsweetened apple juice concentrate
1 teaspoon grated lemon rind
½ cup unsweetened pineapple, crushed, well drained
1 egg white, yolk discarded
¼ cup unsweetened pineapple juice

Preheat the oven to 220°C.
Cover the bottom of the cake tin with a layer of rolled citrus pastry. Save some pastry to make about 10 thin strips for a lattice top.

Filling

Place all the ingredients into a processor and thoroughly mix. Pour the filling onto the pastry. Decorate the top with the 10 pastry strips to form a lattice design. Bake 50 minutes in oven.
  Allow to cool before removing tart from cake tin.
  Serves 4–6.

Variations

MD ## Golden sultana tart

As for Golden Tart but add ½ cup natural sultanas, soaked 1 hour in water and then well drained.

Golden slice   RD

As for Golden Tart but use a 272 x 176 x 35 mm lined slice tin. Spread filling thinly. Bake 15–20 minutes only.

Apple raisin meringue pie   MD

1 sweet pastry flan, medium size, uncooked (see recipe in 'Bread, Scones and Pastries')

Filling

2 cups cooked apples, unsweetened
1 cup raisins, chopped
½ cup water
Grated peel 1 orange
¼ teaspoon cinnamon

Topping

2 egg whites, stiffly beaten, yolks discarded
2 tablespoons canned evaporated skim milk

Preheat the oven to 200°C.

Cook raisins, water and orange peel for 15 minutes. Set aside to cool. When cool, mix thoroughly with cooked apples and cinnamon. Spread evenly onto the pastry flan.

Gently fold canned evaporated skim milk into stiffly beaten egg whites and spread over the top of the apple mixture.

Place the pie in the oven for 15 to 20 minutes, until pastry is cooked and topping is golden brown. Serve hot, topped with More Exchange Cream (see recipe in 'Dips, Dressings and Sauces').

Serves 4–6.

Variation

Apple date meringue pie   MD

As for Apple Raisin Meringue Pie but omit raisins and add ¾ cup chopped pitted dates.

Apple sultana meringue pie   MD

As for Apple Raisin Meringue Pie but omit raisins and add ¾ cup natural sultanas.

Cakes and slices

Banana date cake   MD

2 cups stoneground wholemeal self raising flour
1 cup dates, pitted, halved
½ cup unsweetened dark grape juice
2 bananas, mashed (½ cup)
¼ cup skim milk powder
1½ cups water
¼ teaspoon mixed spice
1 egg white, yolk discarded
¼ teaspoon poppy seeds for topping

Preheat the oven to 230°C. Line square cake tin (195 x 195 x 48 mm) with non-stick paper.

Bring grape juice to the boil in a saucepan, then turn off heat. Add dates. Place lid on and cool. Thoroughly mix all other ingredients except poppy seeds. Add date mixture and pour into a lined square cake tin. Top with poppy seeds.

When cake goes into oven, reduce oven temperature to 180°C and bake for 35 to 40 minutes.

RD
Ginger slice

½ cup crystallized ginger, soaked for 1 hour in boiling water and drained
½ cup apple juice, unsweetened
¼ teaspoon ground ginger
1½ cups stoneground wholemeal self raising flour
¼ cup skim milk powder
1 egg white, yolk discarded
½ cup water
¼ cup unprocessed bran
Cracked wheat for topping

Preheat the oven to 180°C. Line cake tin with non-stick paper.
    Place the drained ginger, apple juice and ground ginger into a saucepan and slowly bring to the boil. Boil for 10 minutes. Cool. Process in a processor and add to the remaining ingredients. Thoroughly mix and spread into lined oblong 272 x 176 x 35 mm tin. Top with cracked wheat. Bake for 20 minutes.
    Remove from the oven and cool, then remove the lining. Cut the cooled slice into squares with electric or very sharp knife.
    Makes about 20 pieces.

Variation

RD
Banana ginger slice

As for Ginger Slice but omit crystallized ginger and add 1 mashed ripe banana.

MD
Banana millet cake

3 dried bananas, chopped (1½ cups) and soaked in boiling water for 1 hour
1 cup grape juice
⅓ cup natural sultanas
¼ cup millet
1 egg white, yolk discarded
¼ cup canned evaporated skim milk, 1 per cent fat maximum
½ cup water
1½ cups stoneground wholemeal self raising flour
1 mashed fresh banana
¼ teaspoon cinnamon

Preheat the oven to 230°C. Line round or square cake tin (213 x 112 x 64 mm) with foil.
    Place dried bananas, grape juice and sultanas in saucepan. Bring to the boil and cool. When cold, blend in blender. Add to remaining ingredients and gently bind together to cake consistency. Place in cake tin.
    Reduce the heat to 180°C when placing the cake in the oven and cook for 1 hour. When cooked place cake in an air tight tin for about 15 to 20 minutes before removing foil.

Sultana slice

MD

½ cup natural sultanas
¼ cup crystallized ginger, soaked for 1 hour in boiling water, drained and chopped
½ cup apple juice, unsweetened
¼ teaspoon mixed spice
1½ cups stoneground wholemeal self raising flour
1 egg white, yolk discarded
¼ cup skim milk powder
½ cup water
¼ cup unprocessed bran
Small quantity of poppy seeds

Sweet pastry, rolled thinly, sufficient to cover the bottom of a 272 x 176 x 35 mm cake tin

Preheat the oven to 180°C. Line cake tin with non-stick paper.

Place the sultanas, chopped ginger, apple juice and mixed spice into saucepan and heat through. Set aside to cool. Thoroughly mix the remaining ingredients and fold in cooled fruit. Press pastry into lined tin and spread mixture over pastry. Top with poppy seeds and bake for 20 minutes. Cool.

Remove from cake tin, remove lining and with electric or sharp knife cut into small pieces. Store in airtight tin.

Makes about 20.

Wheat free 'eggless' Christmas cake

MD

1 cup natural raisins, chopped
1½ cups natural sultanas
1½ cups currants, undipped
1 cup dates, pitted and chopped
8 natural dried apricots, soaked, drained and puréed
⅓ cup mixed peel, soaked 1 hour in boiling water and drained
8 glacé cherries, chopped, soaked 1 hour in boiling water and drained
4 pieces crystallized ginger, finely chopped, soaked 1 hour in boiling water and drained
⅓ cup hulled millet

1 cup water
1 tablespoon whisky or brandy (optional)
¼ cup millet meal
¾ cup barley flour
½ cup buckwheat flour
3 teaspoons baking powder
¾ cup liquid skim milk or water
1 teaspoon nutmeg
½ teaspoon cinnamon
½ teaspoon mixed spice
½ teaspoon sesame seeds

Soak overnight the dried fruit, hulled millet, ginger, cherries, mixed peel and puréed apricots with the cup of water and whisky.

Next day, preheat the oven to 200°C. Line a round or square cake tin (20 or 23 cm) with non-stick paper.

Sift the millet meal, barley flour and buckwheat flour with the baking powder. Sift at least 3 times. Use the residue that collects in the sifter. In a bowl mix the flour, skim milk and spices.

Gradually add the soaked fruit and thoroughly mix to a cake consistency. Pour out into the lined cake tin and cook 30 minutes. Reduce oven temperature to 180°C for 45 minutes and then to 150°C for the remaining 30 minutes. Cool and decorate with Christmas decorations or sesame seeds.

Boiled pineapple fruit cake

MD

1 cup pineapple pieces, unsweetened
1 cup dark unsweetened grape juice
¼ teaspoon mixed spice
½ cup natural sultanas
½ cup currants, undipped
1 cup dates, pitted and chopped

2½ cups stoneground wholemeal self raising flour
1 egg white, yolk discarded
¼ cup skim milk powder
½ cup water

Preheat the oven to 230°C. Line round cake tin (24 cm) with foil.

Boil together the pineapple, grape juice and spice. Set aside and cool. Mix all the remaining ingredients together and gently fold in pineapple mixture. Place into cake tin.

Reduce heat to 180°C when placing cake in oven. Cook for about 40 to 50 minutes.

Carrot cake

MD

1 cup dates, pitted and chopped
1 cup dark grape juice, unsweetened
3 cups carrot, grated
¼ cup canned evaporated skim milk
¼ cup natural sultanas
¼ cup roasted chestnuts, chopped (optional)
⅓ cup unprocessed bran
1 egg white, yolk discarded

2 cups stone ground wholemeal self raising flour
⅓ cup canned evaporated skim milk, 1 per cent fat maximum

Preheat the oven to 230°C. Line cake tin (213 x 112 x 64 mm) with non-stick paper.

Place the dates and grape juice in a saucepan. Bring to the boil, take off heat and add grated carrot. Stir in well and cool. Mix remaining ingredients adding cold date and carrot mixture. Combine well and place in cake tin.

Reduce the heat to 180°C when placing the cake in the oven. Cook 1 hour. Cool and top with 'Creamy' Cheese Frosting (see recipe in 'Dips, Dressings and Sauces').

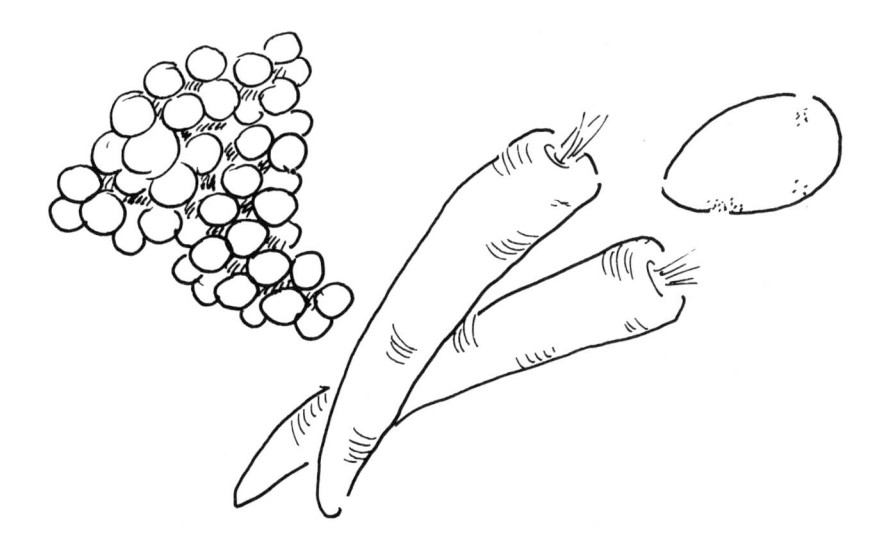

Variation

Spicy carrot cake

MD

As for Carrot Cake but add 1 teaspoon ground mixed spice.

RD ## Cherry delight

1 cup dark cherries, pitted, unsweetened, drained
1 cup stoneground wholemeal self raising flour
1 egg white, yolk discarded
1 tablespoon apple juice concentrate, unsweetened
¼ cup skim milk powder
1 tablespoon canned evaporated skim milk
½ cup water
Small quantity of sesame seeds

½ quantity of Sweet Pastry to cover bottom of square non-stick or lined 195 x 195 x 48 mm square cake tin

Preheat the oven to 230°C. Line cake tin if necessary. Place pastry in tin.

Mix all ingredients except cherries to cake consistency. Pour out about half of the mixture on top of the pastry. Place drained cherries side by side over top of mixture. Pour over the remainder of the cake mixture, covering the cherries as much as possible. Sprinkle over small quantity of sesame seeds.

When cake goes into oven, reduce heat to 180°C. Bake for about 15 to 20 minutes. Remove from oven, when cool cut up into squares.

Makes about 16 squares.

Variations

RD ## Apple delight

As for Cherry Delight but omit cherries and use 1 cup unsweetened apples plus ¼ teaspoon mixed spice.

RD ## Apricot delight

As for Cherry Delight but omit cherries and add 1 cup of chopped unsweetened apricots.

Overleaf: Herbed damper (RD) (page 106), Date and sultana scrolls (MD) (page 105), Salmon paste pinwheels (MD) (page 112).
Spreads in jars: Ginger 'marmalade' (RD) (page 114), Fruit salad chutney (RD) (page 115); in bowl: Dried fig spread (MD) (page 113).

Opposite: Wheat free eggless Christmas cake (MD) (page 96), Fruit tarts (MD) (page 99), using Sweet pastry (RD), Jam tarts with ginger marmalade (RD) (page 99), Summer punch (MD) (page 129)

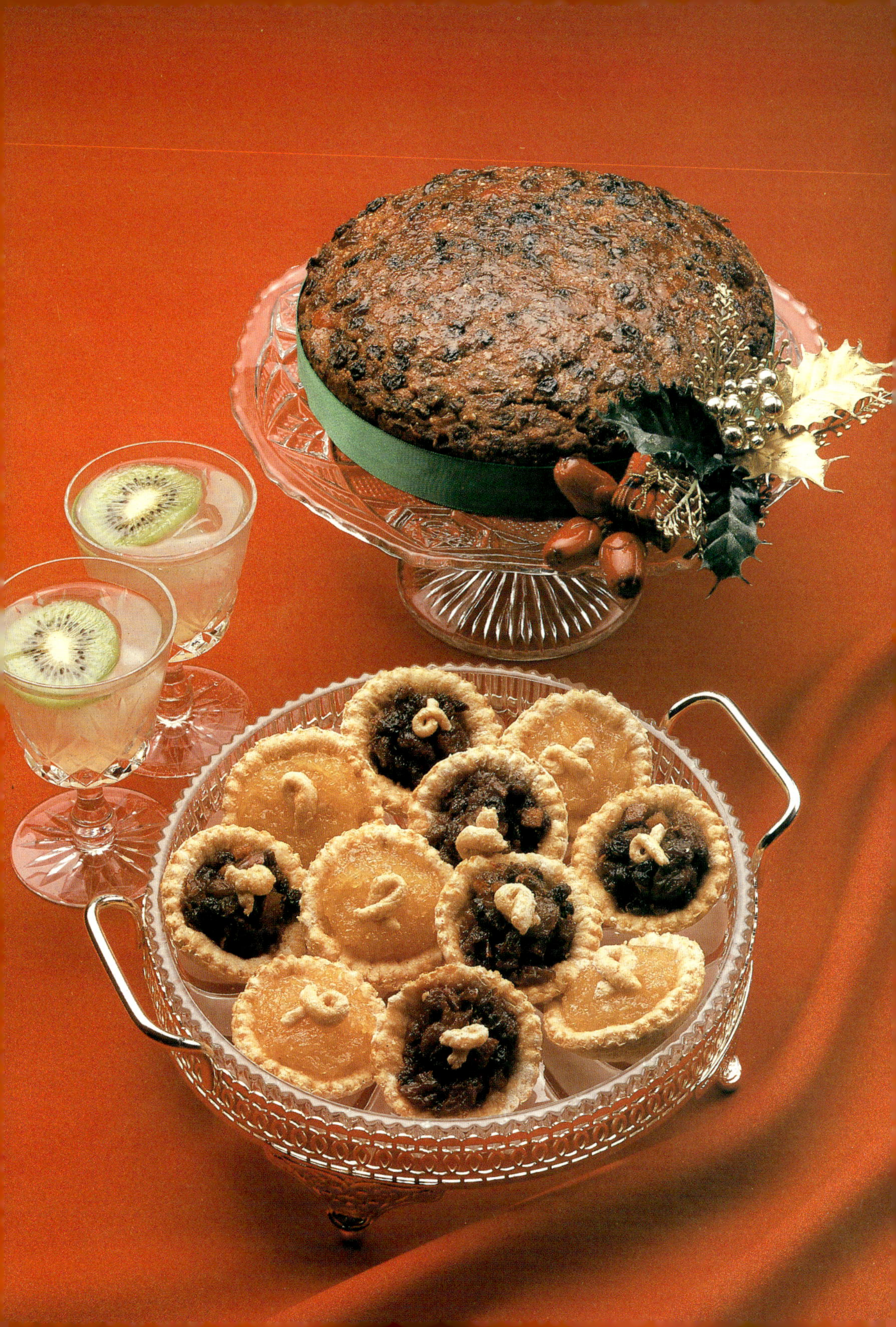

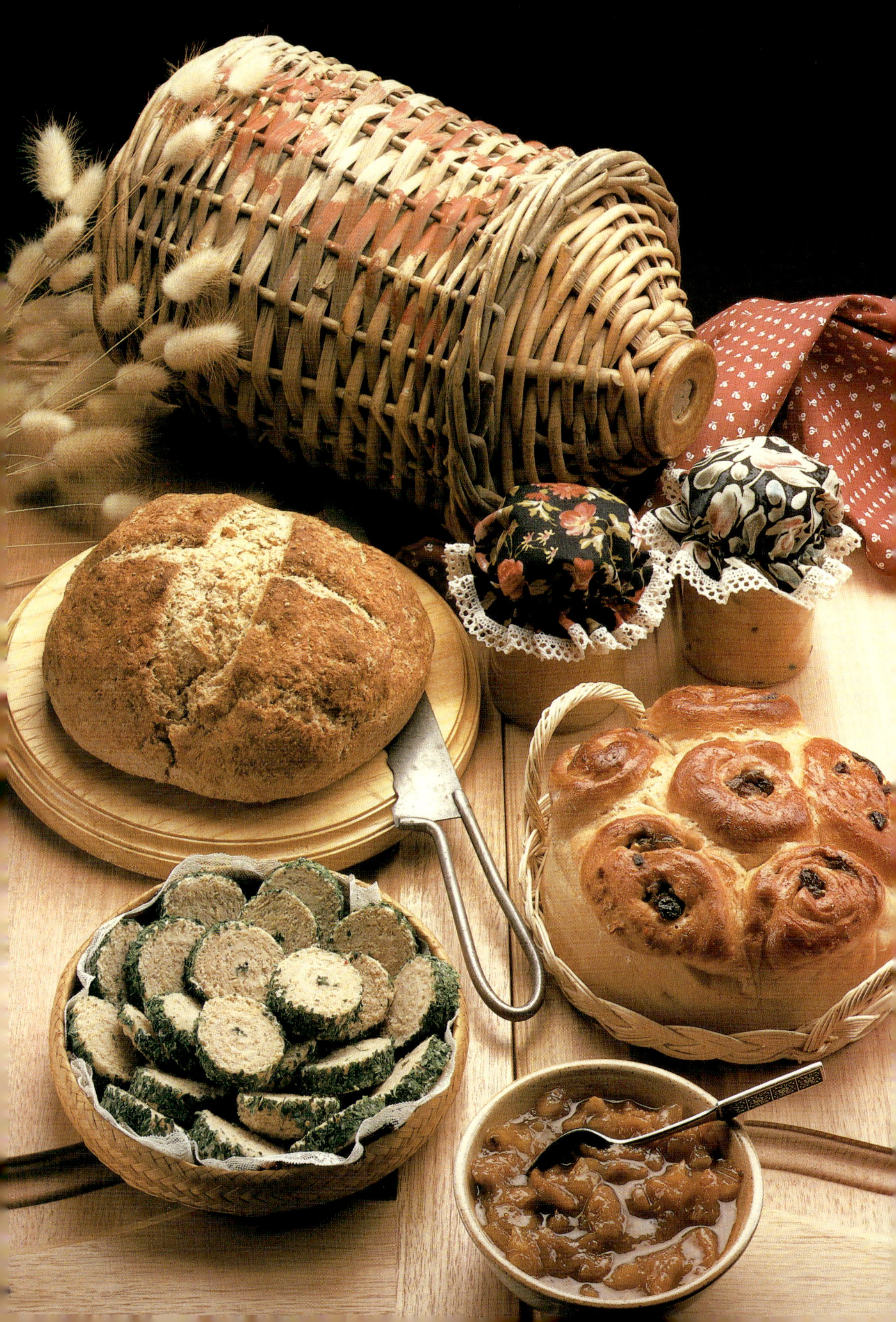

Fruit tarts

MD

½ cup natural sultanas
½ cup currants, undipped
½ cup chopped dates
6 glaće cherries, chopped, soaked for 1 hour in boiling water and drained
1 tablespoon mixed peel, soaked for 1 hour in boiling water and drained
2 tablespoons dark grape juice, unsweetened
½ teaspoon brandy (optional)
1 tablespoon cornflour
1 tablespoon water to mix
1 tablespoon apple juice concentrate

Sweet Pastry to make 12 tarts (see recipe in 'Bread, Scones and Pastries')

Preheat the oven to 180°C.

Place all the fruit, grape juice and brandy into saucepan and slowly heat through. Stir to mix thoroughly. The mixture will dry slightly. Thicken with cornflour and water mixed together. Cool thoroughly.

Pastry

Roll out pastry and cut rounds using large size cutter and place onto non-stick dome patty cake pans, making 12 in all.

Tarts

Fill the 12 pastry lined pans with equal amounts of mixed fruit. Top with folded pastry decoration and lightly brush the pastry with a small quantity of apple juice concentrate.

Place in preheated oven for 15 to 20 minutes until bottoms of tarts are brown.

Makes 12 tarts.

Jam tarts

RD

As for Fruit Tarts but instead of the fruit and grape juice mixture, use any Regressive Diet Fruit Spread of your choice. Watch that spread does not burn during baking. Cool and store tarts in airtight tin. Serve topped with More Exchange Cream (see recipes in 'Dips, Dressings and Sauces').

RD Moist plain chestnut cake

1 cup chestnut purée, no added sugar
¼ cup canned evaporated skim milk, 1 per cent fat maximum
2 tablespoons unsweetened apple juice concentrate
1 egg white, yolk discarded
¾ cup water
1½ cups stoneground wholemeal self raising flour

Topping

½ tablespoon unsweetened apple juice concentrate
½ teaspoon sesame seeds or 'Creamy' Cheese Frosting (see recipe in 'Dips, Dressings and Sauces')

Preheat the oven to 200°C. Line a loaf pan (213 x 112 x 64 mm) with non-stick paper.

Purée together chestnut purée, apple juice concentrate, egg white and evaporated milk until smooth. Gradually mix the flour and water into the purée to make a cake consistency. Pour into the cake tin and bake for 45 minutes.

Topping

If you are decorating the cake with the topping, remove the cake from the oven and brush the top with the apple juice. Decorate with the sesame seeds. Return to the oven for a further 10 minutes.

If you are 'frosting' the cake then allow it to cool first.

This cake is very moist and smooth textured.

Bread, scones and pastries

RD Bread

1 tablespoon active dry yeast
2 teaspoons unsweetened apple
  juice concentrate
2 cups lukewarm water
2 cups stoneground wholemeal
  plain flour
1 cup unbleached white plain
  flour

¼ cup barley flour
¼ cup skim milk powder
Extra stoneground wholemeal flour
A little non-fat yoghurt, sugar-free,
  to brush on top
Cracked wheat or poppy seeds or
  sesame seeds for topping

Preheat the oven to 200°C. Line a bread tin (213 x 112 x 64 mm) with non-stick paper.

Dissolve yeast and apple juice concentrate in the lukewarm water. Thoroughly mix the dry ingredients and add the yeast mixture. Stir well and turn out onto a floured board and knead well, making sure to stretch the dough.

Shape dough into a ball, return to the mixing bowl, cover the bowl with a moist towel and leave in a warm place for 1 hour to allow the dough to rise.

Return the dough to the floured board and knead again with the heel of your hand, once again stretching the dough for about 15 minutes.

Shape the dough into a loaf and place it in the lined tin. Brush lightly with non-fat yoghurt and top with cracked wheat. Cover again with the moist towel, and set aside in a warm place for about 30 minutes.

Place in preheated oven and bake for 1 hour.

Wrap the bread in a clean teatowel for 10 minutes after cooking.

RD Variations

Use the measurements and preparation as for Bread recipe, but vary the types of flour combinations. Always use 3¼ cups of flour.

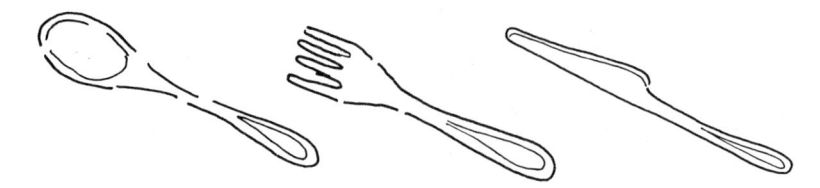

RD Bread rolls

Use the same ingredients and method as for Bread recipe, but after the second kneading shape the bread dough into rolls and continue the rising and cooking method as for bread.

Place in preheated oven and bake for 20–30 minutes.

Makes about 6 rolls.

Croutons

RD

*4 slices approved Pritikin Bread,
  toaster sliced*

Preheat the oven to 140°C.
  Place bread slices flat on a non-stick oven tray and put in the oven for 12 to 15 minutes.
  Take the slices from the oven and with an electric or very sharp knife remove all of the crusts. Cut each slice into about 20 small squares. Arrange these squares again on the non-stick tray and return to the oven for a further 20 minutes. Store in an airtight jar.
  Use as a garnish for soups and salads.

Variations

Garlic croutons

RD

As for Croutons but place the small squares into a plastic bag containing 1 teaspoon garlic powder and toss well. Then proceed as for Coutons.

Onion croutons

RD

As for Croutons but place the small squares into a plastic bag containing 1 teaspoon garlic powder and toss well. Then proceed as for Coutons.

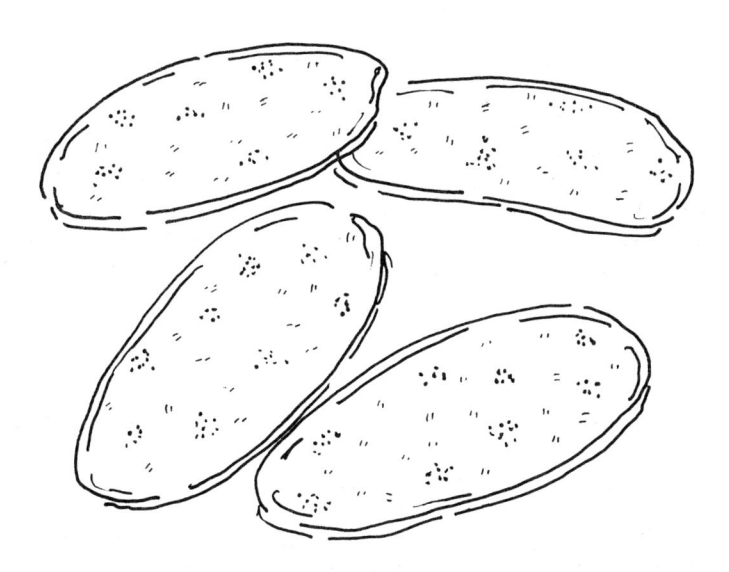

MD # Date and sultana scrolls

Dough

1 tablespoon active dry yeast
1 tablespoon unsweetened apple juice concentrate
2 cups lukewarm water
4 cups stoneground wholemeal plain flour
¼ cup unprocessed bran
Extra stoneground wholemeal flour to knead
¼ cup skim milk powder

Filling

1 cup dates, pitted and chopped
½ cup natural sultanas
¼ cup fresh orange juice

Glaze

Unsweetened apple juice concentrate

Preheat the oven to 210°C. Line a cake tin (20 cm) with non-stick paper.

Dough

Mix yeast, apple juice and lukewarm water. Mix the dry ingredients and add the yeast mixture. Stir well and turn out onto a floured board. Knead really well, making sure to stretch the dough. Shape into a ball, and return to mixing bowl. Cover with a damp towel and leave in a warm place for 1 hour to allow the dough to rise.

Return the dough to the floured board and knead again with the heel of the hand, really stretching the dough.

Shape into a round (19 mm) thick scone and cut the dough into 3 pieces, making one slightly larger than the other two pieces.

Filling

Cook the dates and sultanas in orange juice for 10 minutes, then cool. Divide filling into 3, one portion slightly larger than the other two.

Roll the two smaller pieces of dough into an oblong and spread with the smaller sections of filling. Roll each section up and cut each into 2 pieces.

Stand the 4 scrolls upright and place them side by side around the lined cake tin. Proceed in the same manner with the larger piece, only when it has been spread with the larger remaining filling, roll it up and cut it into 3 scrolls. Place the 3 scrolls into the lined cake tin with one scroll in the middle.

This mixture may be made into 6 if larger scrolls are desired.

Glaze

Brush the tops of the scrolls with a little unsweetened apple juice concentrate.

Cover with a damp towel and place the scrolls in a warm place for a further 20 minutes to allow the dough to rise further.

Place the scrolls into the preheated oven, reducing the temperature to 180°C, for about 1 hour. Tops should be nice and brown.

Makes 7 scrolls.

Variations
Fruit scrolls RD

Follow ingredients and preparation for Date and Sultana Scrolls, but omit filling.

Spread dough with Regression Diet Spread of your choice, and add 1 teaspoon of mixed spice.

Sweet scrolls MD

Follow ingredients and preparation for Date and Sultana Scrolls but omit filling.

Spread dough with a small amount of unsweetened apple juice concentrate and dust with cinnamon.

Date and sultana flour scrolls RD

Follow ingredients and preparation for Date and Sultana Scrolls but use 2 cups stoneground wholemeal plain flour and 2 cups unbleached white plain flour.

Plain muffins RD

2 cups stoneground wholemeal self raising flour
1 tablespoon unsweetened apple juice concentrate
2 tablespoons evaporated skim milk
2 egg whites, yolks discarded
1 cup liquid skim milk
1 teaspoon mixed spice
Cracked wheat for topping

Preheat the oven to 230°C.

Combine all the ingredients and thoroughly mix until the mixture resembles cake consistency. Place large spoonfuls in non-stick muffin trays. Top with cracked wheat.

Reduce the oven temperature to 180°C and bake for 15 to 20 minutes until brown.

Makes about 7 large muffins.

Variation
Orange muffins RD

As for Plain Muffins but use only ½ cup liquid skim milk and add ½ cup fresh orange juice and 1 tablespoon grated orange rind.

RD **Dry bread crumbs**

4 slices approved Pritikin bread or
approved Pritikin bread scraps

Preheat the oven to 140°C.
    Place the bread slices flat on a non-stick oven tray and place in the oven for about 30 minutes, or until bread is dry.
    Remove the tray from the oven and allow bread to cool. Roll bread slices with a rolling pin until each slice is crumbed.
    Store in an airtight jar. Use as a topping.
Makes about 1 cup.

RD **Herbed damper**

4 cups stoneground wholemeal self raising flour
¼ cup evaporated skim milk
1½ cups liquid skim milk
½ teaspoon marjoram
½ teaspoon chopped parsley
A little non-fat yoghurt, sugar free

Extra stoneground wholemeal self raising flour

Preheat the oven to 180°C. Take 1 oven cooking bag, cut along the side and open it out.
    Mix all ingredients thoroughly except non-fat yoghurt and make the mixture into a scone dough. Turn the dough out onto a floured board. Shape dough into a large round scone. Brush top with a little non-fat yoghurt. With a sharp knife cut a shallow cross on the top of the damper. Place damper on a floured non-stick oven tray.
    Bake in oven for 40 to 45 minutes. Ten minutes before removing damper from the oven, wrap it up in the opened out oven cooking bag. Return the wrapped damper for the remaining 10 minutes.
    After removal of the damper from the oven, leave it in the oven cooking bag for a further 15 minutes. This helps to make the top of the damper softer.

Variations

RD **Plain damper**

As for herbed damper but omit the herbs. Add ½ tablespoon unsweetened apple juice concentrate.

Dumplings RD

*1½ cups stoneground wholemeal
  self raising flour*
1 tablespoon skim milk powder
*2 tablespoons canned low fat
  evaporated milk, 1 per cent
  fat maximum*
½ cup water
Extra flour for pastry board

Mix together all the ingredients in a bowl and make a scone dough. Turn out onto a pastry board and form the dough into a large scone. With a small scone cutter, cut into 6 dumplings.

Gently place dumplings on the top of the casserole and cook 15 minutes each side.

Variations

Herbed dumplings RD

As for Dumplings but add ½–1 teaspoon of mixed herbs and a pinch of cayenne pepper.

Sesame dumplings RD

As for Dumplings but add ¼ teaspoon of sesame seeds to the mixture.

RD # Sprouted brown rice scones

2 cups stoneground wholemeal self raising flour
¼ cup sprouted brown rice (2–3 days growth only)
½ tablespoon unsweetened apple juice concentrate
2 tablespoons evaporated skim milk, 1 per cent fat maximum
¾ cup water

A little non-fat yoghurt to brush tops of scones or *a little unsweetened apple juice concentrate*
Extra stoneground wholemeal self raising flour

Preheat the oven to 230°C.
    Mix all the ingredients into a scone dough. Turn out onto a floured board. Knead lightly and shape into a large round scone. Cut into scones with a round cutter.
    Brush the tops with topping of choice.
    Place on a non-stick tray or tray lined with non-stick paper. Cook in the oven 10 to 12 minutes.
    Makes about 8 scones.

RD # Sprouted bread

2 cups sprouted wheat (3 days' growth)
Preheat the oven to 120°C.
Rinse the sprouts well, drain and place in a food mill and grind.
    Shape the mixture into a small loaf. Place in a lined loaf tin (small) and bake very slowly for 1½ to 2 hours until top is brown and bread cooked.
    Although this bread is fairly doughy it is very tasty and extremely nutritious.
    Makes about 4 small slices.

Plain pastry

RD

1 cup unbleached white plain flour
¼ cup stoneground wholemeal self raising flour
2 tablespoons evaporated skim milk
⅓ cup and 1 tablespoon liquid skim milk
Extra stoneground wholemeal self raising flour

Mix all of the dry ingredients, then add the liquids to make a pastry dough.

Use the extra flour to roll out the dough. Knead lightly and roll the dough as desired.

Note: Always lift the rolled pastry off the board and put it back on the board before cutting. This allows the pastry to shrink. Then cut into the sizes required.

Variation

Herbed pastry

RD

As for Plain Pastry but add ½ teaspoon mixed herbs.

Sweet pastry

RD

1 cup unbleached white plain flour
¼ cup stoneground wholemeal self raising flour
2 tablespoons evaporated skim milk
⅓ cup and 1 tablespoon unsweetened apple juice
Extra stoneground wholemeal self raising flour

Follow recipe for Plain Pastry.
Makes approximately 14 small tart bases.

Citrus pastry

RD

1 cup unbleached white plain flour
¼ cup stoneground wholemeal self raising flour
½ tablespoon unsweetened apple juice concentrate
1 tablespoon lemon juice
1 teaspoon grated lemon peel
1 tablespoon evaporated skim milk
⅓ cup water
Extra stoneground wholemeal self raising flour

Mix all of the ingredients together to make a pastry dough. Knead lightly. Use the extra flour to roll out the pastry.

RD **Yeast pastry**

1½ teaspoons active dry yeast
1 cup warm skim milk liquid
1 cup unbleached white plain flour

1 cup stoneground wholemeal plain flour
Extra stoneground wholemeal flour

Thoroughly dissolve the yeast with the warm skim milk. Mix together both flours. Make a well in the centre and pour in the mixed yeast and milk. Form a dough and knead very well for at least 15 minutes, stretching the dough as much as possible.

Form the dough into a ball and place back into the bowl. Cover with a moist towel and place in a warm position until double its size — about ¾ hour.

Return to the floured board, knead again for about 10 minutes. Pastry is ready to use.

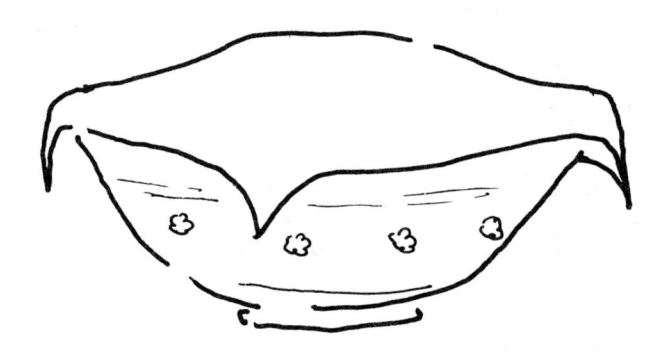

RD **Potato pastry**

1 cup stoneground wholemeal self raising flour
½ cup unbleached white plain flour
¼ cup potato flour
¾ cup liquid skim milk

Extra stoneground wholemeal self raising flour

Follow recipe for Plain Pastry.

Basic pikelets　　　　　　　　　　　　　　　　　　RD

1 cup stoneground wholemeal
　self raising flour
¼ skim milk powder
1 cup water

1 teaspoon vanilla essence
(omit if savoury pikelets
are desired)

Mix together the flour and skim milk powder. Slowly add the water to mix into a paste — the mixture will be thin at first. Leave it to stand for about 15 minutes and it will thicken until ready to use.

Drop spoonfuls onto a fairly hot non-stick frying pan. Cook pikelets and turn over when upper side bubbles. Use a plastic slide so as not to damage the surface of the non-stick pan.

Serve as a savoury or top with unsweetened spread and top with More Exchange Cream (see recipe in 'Dips, Dressings and Spreads').

Makes about 15 pikelets.

Variations

Sweet pikelets　　　　　　　　　　　　　　　　　　RD

As for Basic Pikelets but add 1 tablespoon unsweetened apple juice concentrate.

Date pikelets　　　　　　　　　　　　　　　　　　MD

As for Sweet Pikelets but add ½ cup chopped pitted dates.

Raisin pikelets　　　　　　　　　　　　　　　　　　MD

As for Sweet Pikelets but add ½ cup natural raisins, chopped.

Sultana pikelets　　　　　　　　　　　　　　　　　　MD

As for Sweet Pikelets but add ½ cup natural sultanas.

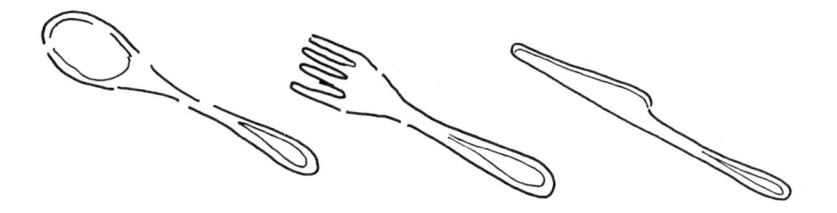

RD **Fruit pikelets**

1 cup stoneground wholemeal self raising flour
¼ cup skim milk powder
¾ cup water
1 teaspoon vanilla essence

½ cup chopped fresh fruit of choice, for example, mashed banana, grated fresh apple, chopped strawberries, mashed apricots

Thoroughly mix all the ingredients. Drop spoonfuls in a non-stick pan, then when first side bubbles, turn over and cook the other side.

Eat hot or topped with More Exchange Cream (see recipes in 'Dips, Dressings and Sauces') or Vanilla Custard (see recipe this section).

Makes about 12.

MD **Salmon paste pinwheels**

3 slices of approved Pritikin bread, sliced longways *not* across
½ cup Salmon Paste (see recipe in 'Spreads, Chutneys and Pastes')
Small quantity of low fat skim milk cottage cheese, 1 per cent fat maximum

A little skim milk
Small quantity of dried parsley

Cut off the crusts from each slice of bread and gently roll each slice with a rolling pin until reasonably thin.

Gently spread one side of each slice of bread with the Salmon Paste and tightly roll up each slice across until it resembles a small log. Roll up each log in plastic wrap and refrigerate about 4 hours.

Remove from the refrigerator, and take off the plastic wrap. Lightly spread the outside of each log with a paste made from the cottage cheese and skim milk and coat each log with dried parsley.

With an electric knife slice each log into about 6 rounds trimming both ends before you start to cut. Arrange on a platter and serve.

Makes about 18 rounds.

Spreads, chutneys and pastes

'Dried fig' spread
MD

8 dried figs, soaked ½ hour in boiling water, drained and chopped
1 cup unsweetened apple juice

3 pieces crystallized ginger, soaked 1 hour in boiling water then chopped

Place all prepared ingredients into saucepan, bring to boil and gently simmer ¾ hour until thick and looking like jam.
 Cool and place in sterilized jars and refrigerate.
 Makes about 1¼ cups.

RD ## Fig and ginger spread

6 pieces glacé ginger, soaked 1 hour in boiling water, drained and chopped

10 medium to large figs, ripe

Wash figs thoroughly, remove stems, and slice into chunks. Place with chopped ginger into saucepan (lid on) and very slowly bring to the boil. Gently simmer ½–1 hour. Stir occasionally. Remove lid and simmer further ¾ hour. Continue to stir occasionally. Mixture should be fairly thick.

Cool and place in sterilized jars.

Makes about 1½ cups.

RD ## Ginger 'marmalade'

1 cup crystallized ginger (not cut), soaked 1 hour in boiling water and drained
1 cup water

¼ cup unsweetened apple juice
1 teaspoon cornflour with extra water to mix

Mix cornflour with water and set aside.

Place remaining ingredients into a saucepan and gently simmer ¾ hour. Remove and process finely in processor.

Return to saucepan and thicken with cornflour. Simmer further 15 minutes. Store in sterilized jar in refrigerator.

Makes about ¾ cup.

RD ## Plum spread

6 blood plums, chopped into chunks

½ cup unsweetened apple juice

Place plums and apple juice into saucepan (lid on) and slowly bring to the boil. Gently simmer for 1½ hours until mixture is thick and spreadable. Remove lid after 1 hour.

Cool and place in sterilized jars.

Makes about 1 cup.

RD ## Quince spread

4 medium to large quinces

¼ cup unsweetened apple juice

Peel quinces, cut into slices and place in a saucepan with apple juice. Slowly bring to the boil and gently simmer. Stir occasionally for about 1 to 1½ hours or until it becomes a spreadable consistency.

Suitable for use in pies or as a dessert with yoghurt or Cream Exchange (see recipe in 'Dips, Dressings and Sauces').

Variation
Quince and apple spread   RD

As for Quince Spread but omit 1 quince and add 2 peeled sliced cooking apples.

Tomato spread   RD

1 tomato, chopped
1 onion, chopped
¾ cup water
¼ cup unsweetened apple juice concentrate

1 cup tomato paste, no added salt
1 teaspoon garlic granules
2 teaspoons sweet basil
2 teaspoons oregano

Prepare and place all ingredients into a medium saucepan and gently simmer for about 1 hour. Place into processor and process fine.
Cool and place in sterilized jars and refrigerate.
Use as a sandwich spread or in cooking as a pizza topping.
Makes about 1½ cups.

Variation
Tomato spread with grape juice   MD

As for Tomato Spread but omit water and use ¾ cup unsweetened grape juice.

Fruit salad chutney   RD

1 small apple, peeled, chopped finely
1½ cups pawpaw, chopped finely
1 medium pear, peeled, chopped
1 cup sultana grapes
2 passionfruit, pulp only
1 clove garlic, chopped finely
⅓ cup vinegar

½ cup unsweetened apple juice
¼ teaspoon powdered ginger

Prepare and place all ingredients in saucepan (lid on). Bring slowly to the boil. Remove lid and gently simmer 1 to 1½ hours.
Cool and place in sterilized jars. Seal, store in refrigerator. It is best to use this chutney when freshly cooked. It will keep for a longer time if frozen in airtight plastic containers. Reheat after thawing.
Makes about 1½ cups.

MD ## Mango and pawpaw chutney

1 mango, peeled and chopped
½ medium pawpaw, peeled and chopped
1 medium onion, chopped
¼ teaspoon powdered ginger
¼ teaspoon garlic powder
½ cup unsweetened apple juice
⅓ cup dates, pitted and finely chopped
⅓ cup Ezy Sauce or Spiced Vinegar (see recipe this section)

Prepare and place all ingredients in saucepan (lid on). Slowly bring to the boil. Remove lid and gently simmer 1½ hours.

Cool and place in sterilized jars. Store in refrigerator or freeze for longer storage.

MD ## Round beef paste

50 g lean round beef, cooked, all fat removed
1 tablespoon low fat skim milk cottage cheese, 1 per cent fat maximum
1 teaspoon liquid skim milk
Pinch garlic powder
Pinch ground nutmeg
½ tablespoon chives, chopped

Place beef, cottage cheese and skim milk in a processor and process using cutting blade until meat is shredded.

Remove from the processor and gently mix with the remaining ingredients.

Use as a sandwich filling.

Makes about ½ cup.

MD **Variation**

As for Round Beef Paste but add 2 tablespoons Tomato Sauce (see recipe in *It's Only Natural*).

MD ## Mango chutney

3 large firm mangoes, peeled, thinly sliced
1 cup white vinegar
½ cup date purée (see recipe in It's Only Natural)
1 cup natural sultanas
1 clove garlic, chopped finely
¼ cup fresh ginger, grated
1 small red chilli, seeded and chopped

Stand mango slices overnight, and drain off any fluid.

Next day combine vinegar and date purée in saucepan, bring to boil and simmer for 5 minutes. Add mangoes and remaining ingredients. Simmer a further hour or until chutney is a good consistency.

Cool and place in sterilized jars and seal. Store in refrigerator.

Makes about 2 cups.

'Mock' turkey   RD

1 small tomato, peeled and sliced
2 teaspoons mixed herbs
1 teaspoon sapsago cheese
1 slice approved Pritikin bread, crusts removed
½ small onion, chopped
½ tablespoon Quick Tomato Sauce (see recipe in 'Dips, Dressings and Sauces')

Cook tomato and onion in non-stick saucepan until onion is soft. Add the mixed herbs and sapsago cheese, stir well.

Place the mixture and bread into a processor, using the cutting blade, and process until mixture is a fairly smooth paste. Add the tomato sauce and stir well.

Place in a container and refrigerate. Use cold as a sandwich filling.
Makes about ¾ cup.

Salmon paste   MD

100 g pink salmon, skin and bones removed and rinsed under tap to remove brine
1 teaspoon vinegar
1 tablespoon low fat skim milk cottage cheese, 1 per cent fat maximum

Thoroughly blend all the ingredients in a processor, using cutting blade, until the mixture resembles a paste.

Use as a sandwich filling.
Makes about ½ cup.

Green tomato pickles   MD

1 kg green tomatoes, sliced thinly
300 g onions, sliced thinly
1 cup unsweetened apple juice
1 cup dates, pitted
1 teaspoon turmeric
½ cup Ezy Sauce or Spiced Vinegar (see recipe this section)
1½ tablespoons cornflour with extra water to mix

Place sliced tomatoes and onions in a large bowl, cover and stand overnight. Pour off any liquid next day.

Place in large saucepan. Bring to the boil very slowly (lid on). Gently simmer occasionally stirring for about 1 hour.

Cook dates in apple juice and blend with tomatoes and onions. Add Ezy Sauce or Spiced Vinegar and gently simmer a further hour with lid off. Add cornflour and turmeric mixed with water.

Allow to cool and place in sterilized jars. Cover and store in refrigerator. These pickles will only keep a few weeks, but you can freeze them and reheat before using.
Makes approximately 4½ cups.

MD ## Spiced vinegar

2 cups white vinegar
1 dessertspoon peppercorns
1 teaspoon cloves, whole
1 teaspoon wholespice
⅛ teaspoon cayenne pepper

This Spiced Vinegar is intended for use in savoury sauce recipes such as the Tomato Sauce recipes in *It's Only Natural* or the Quick Tomato Sauce in 'Dips, Dressings and Sauces' in this book.

Tie peppercorns, cloves and wholespice in a small calico bag. Add bag and cayenne pepper to vinegar and place into sauce after mixture has cooked. Cook 1 hour and remove spice bag just before bottling sauce.

MD ## Pickled onions

About 40 small pickling onions
Quantity of unsweetened apple juice
6 cups vinegar
½ bottle Ezy Sauce
2 teaspoons peppercorns
1 teaspoon cloves, whole
1 teaspoon wholespice

Top, tail and peel onions. Place into glass or plastic bowl and cover with apple juice. Cover and leave to stand about 36 to 48 hours. After 48 hours drain off apple juice and discard.

Place peppercorns, cloves and wholespice in calico bag. Boil Ezy Sauce, vinegar and spices. Add onions to boiling pickling mixture for 10 minutes.

Allow to cool.

Place onions in sterilized glass jars. Cover with vinegar mixture and cover jars.

Makes around 3 jars.

Dips, dressings and sauces

Tarragon dressing
RD

¼ cup canned evaporated skim milk, 1 per cent fat maximum
1 rounded tablespoon non-fat uncreamed cottage cheese
1 tablespoon lemon juice
2 tablespoons tarragon vinegar
¼ teaspoon dry mustard
1 tablespoon skim milk liquid
½ teaspoon dried tarragon leaves

Thoroughly mix all the ingredients in a processor or blender until smooth.
   Makes approximately ½ cup.

Mustard and vinegar dressing
RD

½ tablespoon dry mustard
1 tablespoon unsweetened apple juice
½ cup vinegar

Mix the mustard with the apple juice and slowly add the vinegar. Stir constantly until the dressing is smooth.
   Makes about ½ cup.

RD ## Special French dressing

¼ teaspoon dry mustard
¼ teaspoon paprika
⅓ cup white vinegar
1 tablespoon wine vinegar
1 small clove garlic, crushed
1 teaspoon unsweetened apple juice concentrate

1 tablespoon lemon juice
Grated rind 1 lemon
Dash freshly ground black pepper (optional)

Blend mustard and paprika with a little vinegar, then thoroughly mix together all the ingredients.
Makes about ½ cup.

Variation

RD ## Dill dressing

As for Special French Dressing but add ½ teaspoon dried dill.

RD ## Thousand island dressing

⅓ cup non-fat yoghurt, sugar free
⅓ cup Quick Tomato Sauce (see recipe in this section)
1 tablespoon unsweetened apple juice concentrate

1 tablespoon vinegar
1½ tablespoons lemon juice
2 tablespoons liquid skim milk
½ teaspoon mustard powder

Thoroughly mix all the ingredients in a processor or blender until smooth.
Makes approximately 1 cup.

MD ## Corn and tuna dip

½ cup low fat skim milk cottage cheese, 1 per cent fat maximum
½ cup low fat ricotta cheese, 1 per cent fat maximum
2 tablespoons liquid skim milk
3 tablespoons dried onions, finely chopped
½ teaspoon unsweetened apple juice concentrate

¾ cup fresh corn kernels, steamed
½ cup flaked tuna, skin and bones removed, rinsed in water
3 tablespoons dried parsley, chopped

Thoroughly mix all the ingredients except parsley, corn and tuna in a blender. Fold in the corn and tuna. Fold in the parsley. Chill in refrigerator.
Serve with fresh salad vegetables or approved crackers.
Makes about 2 cups.

Creamy mayonnaise   RD

¼ cup canned evaporated skim milk, 1 per cent fat maximum
1 rounded tablespoon non-fat uncreamed cottage cheese
1 tablespoon lemon sauce
1 tablespoon vinegar
¼ teaspoon dry mustard
½ tablespoon unsweetened apple juice concentrate
Extra skim milk

Place all the ingredients in a blender or processor and mix until smooth. Add extra skim milk if too thick.

This mayonnaise may need to be mixed again if stored in refrigerator more than 24 hours before using.

Makes about ½ cup.

Variation

Soy sauce dressing   RD

As for Creamy Mayonnaise but add ¼ teaspoon soy sauce, low salt.

Mayonnaise 2   RD

½ cup non-fat yoghurt, sugar free
1 tablespoon unsweetened apple juice concentrate
¼ cup vinegar
1 tablespoon lemon juice
1 teaspoon powdered skim milk
1 teaspoon dry mustard
1 tablespoon water

Place all the ingredients into a blender or processor and mix until smooth.
Makes 1 cup.

Curried egg sandwich filling   RD

2 egg whites, hard boiled, yolks discarded
¼ teaspoon curry powder
1 tablespoon canned evaporated skim milk, 1 per cent fat maximum
Pinch dried parsley (optional)

Mash the egg whites in a dish with a fork, add the curry powder and milk. Mix well.

Makes filling for 4 rounds of Pritikin sandwiches.

Variation

As for Curried Egg Sandwich Filling but add small amounts of finely shredded lettuce *or* a small amount of alfalfa sprouts.

RD ## 'Creamy' cheese frosting

½ cup low fat skim milk cottage cheese, 1 per cent fat maximum
1 tablespoon canned evaporated skim milk, 1 per cent fat maximum
1 tablespoon unsweetened apple juice concentrate

Blend together all the ingredients in a processor until thoroughly mixed and smooth.

RD **Variations**

As for 'Creamy' Cheese Frosting but add ½ teaspoon grated lemon rind and ½ teaspoon lemon juice.

As for 'Creamy' Cheese Frosting but omit evaporated milk and add ½ teaspoon grated orange rind and 1 tablespoon fresh orange juice.

As for 'Creamy' Cheese Frosting but add ¼ cup chestnut purée.

RD ## White sauce

1 tablespoon canned evaporated skim milk, 1 per cent fat maximum
2 cups skim milk liquid
¼ cup unbleached plain flour

Thoroughly mix flour with enough milk to make a paste. Gradually mix in remaining skim milk in a saucepan. Gently and slowly bring to the boil stirring constantly until thickened.

If a thicker sauce is required add extra unbleached flour to the mixture at beginning of mixing.

Makes approximately 2½ cups.

Variations

RD As for White Sauce but replace 1 cup of liquid skim milk with
1 cup beef stock, defatted
or
1 cup chicken stock, defatted
or
1 cup fish or vegetable stock, defatted
or
1 tablespoon of dry white wine.

Sweet 'n sour sauce   RD

1 tablespoon arrowroot with extra water to mix
1 cup unsweetened pineapple juice
1 tablespoon unsweetened apple juice concentrate
1 tablespoon lemon juice
1 tablespoon Quick Tomato Sauce (see recipe in this section)
1 tablespoon tomato paste, salt free
1 teaspoon soy sauce, low salt
1 teaspoon sesame seeds (optional)

Thoroughly blend together arrowroot and water. Add all remaining ingredients and stir well. Mixture is now ready to be added to other dishes for cooking. Cook about 15 minutes to thicken.
Makes about 1½ cups.

Mushroom dip   RD

1 cup low fat cottage cheese, 1 per cent fat maximum
½ cup button mushrooms, finely chopped
1 tablespoon chives, chopped
1 teaspoon unsweetened apple juice concentrate
½ teaspoon chilli seasoning
½ teaspoon poppy seeds to garnish

Blend together all the ingredients and chill in the refrigerator until required. Top with poppy seeds.
Serve with fresh vegetables on approved crackers.

More exchange cream 1   RD

1 cup ricotta cheese, non-fat, 1 per cent fat maximum
3 tablespoons canned evaporated skim milk, 1 per cent fat maximum
1 teaspoon vanilla essence
½ cup skim milk liquid

Thoroughly mix together all ingredients in a processor or blender until smooth.
Makes approximately 2 cups.

Variation

Sweet more exchange cream   RD

As for More Exchange Cream 1 but add ½ tablespoon unsweetened apple juice concentrate.

RD ## More exchange cream 2

¼ cup non-fat uncreamed cottage cheese
¼ cup canned evaporated skim milk, 1 per cent fat maximum
½ tablespoon unsweetened apple juice concentrate
½ teaspoon vanilla essence (optional)

Thoroughly mix together all ingredients in a processor or blender until smooth. This cream may need to be mixed again if stored in refrigerator for more than 24 hours.

MD ## Plum sauce 1

300 g blood plums
½ cup dates, pitted
1 medium onion, chopped
½ cup cider vinegar, or
⅛ teaspoon chilli powder
½ cup Ezy Sauce or Spiced Vinegar (see recipes in this section)
½ teaspoon ground ginger

Wash and dry plums, and remove stones. Place plums, dates and onion into saucepan (lid on). Bring to boil slowly and simmer ¾ hour. Remove lid after ½ hour. Add remaining ingredients after ¾ hour.

Place in blender and blend until smooth.

Return to heat, simmer further ½ to ¾ hour. Cool and place in sterilized jars. Keeps several months.

Makes about 1 cup.

RD ## Plum sauce 2

400 g blood plums

Wash and dry plums, remove stones. Place plums into saucepan (lid on). Slowly bring to the boil and gently simmer ½ hour. Remove lid and gently simmer a further ½ hour until thick. Keeps about 2 weeks in refrigerator.

Makes about 1 cup.

RD ## Chestnut whip

¼ cup chestnut purée, no added sugar
¼ cup non-fat uncreamed cottage cheese
¼ cup skim milk liquid
1 tablespoon unsweetened apple juice concentrate

Thoroughly combine all ingredients in a processor until smooth.

Refrigerate about 10 to 16 hours to thicken, then use.

Use as a topping on desserts or on sliced cake as it is served.

Makes good ½ cup.

Fruit whip RD

3/4 cup non-fat yoghurt, sugar free
2 tablespoons skim milk powder
1 tablespoon unsweetened apple
 juice concentrate
Pinch cinnamon
1/4 cup fresh fruit of choice, for
 example, banana, pears, apricots,
 berries
1/2 teaspoon vanilla (optional)

Thoroughly mix together all ingredients in a processor or blender until smooth. Serve chilled over your favourite dessert or as a dip.
Makes approximately 1 1/2 cups.

Marinade for meat RD

This marinade is suitable for Regression Diet usage. However, it must be remembered that 100 g is the maximum meat allowance per week. This marinade may be used to flavour the serving.

1 cup vinegar
1 cup dry white wine
1/4 teaspoon rosemary
1/4 teaspoon marjoram
1 tablespoon dried parsley flakes
1 bay leaf
1/4 teaspoon peppercorns

Mix together all ingredients and use as a marinade for beef or chicken. Refrigerate until used.

Remove bay leaf and peppercorns just before cooking the meat and marinade.
Makes about 2 cups.

Seasoned flour 1 RD

2 tablespoons stoneground
 wholemeal plain flour
1 teaspoon dry mustard
1 teaspoon curry powder
1/4 teaspoon ginger powder

Place all of the ingredients into a medium sized plastic bag. Shake well to mix. It is now ready to use.
Will coat 300 to 400 g meat, fish or chicken.

Seasoned flour 2 RD

2 tablespoons stoneground
 wholemeal plain flour
1 teaspoon dry mustard
1 teaspoon curry powder
1/4 teaspoon garlic powder

Place all of the ingredients into a medium sized plastic bag. Shake well to mix. It is now ready to use.
Will coat 300 to 400 g meat, fish or chicken.

RD ## Quick tomato sauce

1 cup water
1 medium sized onion, chopped
2 cloves garlic, crushed
1 cup tomato paste, salt free
2 tablespoons unsweetened apple juice concentrate

½ cup Ezy Sauce or Spiced Vinegar (see recipe in this section)

Gently simmer water, onion and garlic in a saucepan (lid on) until onion is soft. Add the tomato paste, stir thoroughly and process the mixture in a processor until puréed. Return the mixture to the saucepan. Add the remaining ingredients, mix thoroughly and simmer over a very low heat for 15 to 20 minutes.
    Cool slightly, pour into a sterilized jar or bottle.
Makes about 2½ cups.

RD ## Seasoned sweet sauce

Use either the ingredients for Seasoned Flour 1 or ingredients for Seasoned Flour 2 (see recipes in this section)
1 cup water

½–1 tablespoon unsweetened apple juice concentrate

Preparation 1

Mix all the ingredients together making sure to mix the dry ingredients thoroughly. Place in a saucepan and gradually bring to the boil and stir constantly. Simmer gently until the sauce is thick.

Preparation 2

Mix all the ingredients together making sure that the dry ingredients are thoroughly mixed.
    Pour over the vegetables that are cooking and gently stir as the mixture thickens.

Variation

MD Follow one of the preparations for Seasoned Sweet Sauce but omit apple juice concentrate and use ½ cup unsweetened fruit juice of choice with ½ cup water.

Beverages

Basic vanilla milk shake   RD

2 cups skim milk liquid, very slightly frozen
1 tablespoon unsweetened apple juice concentrate
¼ cup canned evaporated skim milk, 1 per cent fat maximum
¼ teaspoon vanilla essence

Grated nutmeg for topping

Blend together all the ingredients in a processor until thick and creamy. Pour into long glasses and top with a little grated nutmeg.
Makes 3 cups.

Variation

Strawberry milk shake   RD

As for Basic Vanilla Milk Shake, but add ½ cup fresh strawberries.

Fruit milk shake   RD

As for Basic Vanilla Milk Shake but add ½ cup of fresh fruit of choice.

Grape juice and apple toddy   MD

2 cups unsweetened grape juice
2 cups unsweetened apple juice
2 cups sparkling mineral water

Strawberries to decorate

Mix together all the ingredients and serve in small stemmed glasses over crushed ice. Decorate each drink with a strawberry on a tooth pick.
Makes 6 cups.

MD ## Summer punch

2 pieces of glacé ginger, soaked 1 hour in boiling water and drained
Two 450 g cans unsweetened pineapple juice
1 bottle mineral water

1 kiwi fruit, peeled and sliced

Purée soaked ginger in a processor using cutting blade and mix with pienapple juice and mineral water. Float kiwi fruit on top.
Makes sufficient for a party.

RD ## Tomato cocktail

2 cups tomato juice, no added salt or sugar
½ tablespoon lemon juice
Cucumber or lemon slices to decorate

1 cup sparkling mineral water

Mix together and serve over crushed ice.
Makes 4 small glasses.

RD ## Vegetable juice quencher

2 cups vegetable juice, no added salt or sugar
½ tablespoon soy sauce, low salt
Pinch garlic powder

Lemon slices to decorate

Mix together all the ingredients and serve over crushed ice.
Makes about 2 cups.

Index

Apple and carrot salad (RD) 45
Apple date meringue pie (MD) 91
Apple delight (RD) 98
Apple raisin meringue pie (MD) 91
Apple sultana meringue pie (MD) 91
Apricot delight (RD) 98
Artichokes (globe) (RD) 53
Asparagus morany flan (RD) 54
Au gratin potatoes (RD) 55
Baked fish asparagus (MD) 79
Baked fish casserole (MD) 79
Baked pears and rice (RD) 82
Banana custard (RD) 82
Banana date cake (MD) 93
Banana ginger slice (RD) 94
Banana millet cake (MD) 94
Basic pikelets (RD) 111
Basic vanilla milk shake (RD) 127
Beef stock 38
Beef and barley soup (RD) 39
Beef stew, 'Seasoned' (MD) 74 with dumplings (MD) 73
Beetroot, jellied (RD) 48
Beetroot and apple salad (RD) 46
Beetroot and pineapple salad (RD) 46
Beverages 127–129
Boiled pineapple fruit cake (MD) 96
Brandy banana custard (RD) 82
Bread (RD) 102
Bread rolls (RD) 102
Bread, scones and pastries 101–112
Broccoli and cauliflower mornay (RD) 55
Brussels sprouts (RD) 56
Cakes and slices 93–100
Candied sweet potatoes (RD) 55
Cannelloni (RD) 63
Capsicum beef (MD) 71
Caraway slaw (MD) 47
Carob-flavoured 'ice-cream' (RD) 83
Carrot cake (MD) 97

Carrot cake, spicy (MD) 97
Cherry delight (RD) 98
Cherry, grape and pineapple salad (RD) 47
Chestnut whip (RD) 124
Chicken, curried (MD) 78
Chicken à l'orange (MD) 77
Chicken and rice soup (MD) 39
Chicken and rice soup, curried (MD) 38
Chicken in soy sauce (MD) 76
Chicken stock 37
Chicken vegetable surprise (MD) 76
Chinese 'stir fried' beef (MD) 70
Christmas cake 96
Chunky island vegetable sauté (RD) 57
Citrus pastry (RD) 109
Corn and carrot pudding (RD) 56
Corn and potato salad (RD) 47
Corn and tuna dip (MD) 120
Cream of chicken soup (MD) 44
Cream of left-over soup (RD) 43
Cream of lobster soup (MD) 44
Cream of prawn soup (MD) 43
Creamed corn (RD) 59
Creamed fish pan style (MD) 78
Creamed rice again (RD) 84
Creamed rice pudding (RD) 83
Creamed sago (RD) 84
'Creamy' cheese frosting (RD) 122
Creamy mayonnaise (RD) 121
Croutons (RD) 103; garlic (RD) 103; onion (RD) 103
Cucumber special (RD) 49
Curried cabbage (RD) 61
Curried chicken (MD) 78
Curried chicken and rice soup (MD) 38
Curried egg sandwich filling (RD) 121
Curried ground beef (MD) 70
Curried left-over soup (RD) 43
Curried salmon patties (MD) 80
Curried vegetable casserole (RD) 61

Date pikelets (MD) 111
Date and sultana flour scrolls (RD) 105
Date and sultana scrolls (MD) 104
Deluxe coleslaw (RD) 50
Desserts 81–92
Dill dressing (RD) 120
Dips, dressings and sauces 119–126
'Dried fig' spread (MD) 113
Dry bread crumbs (RD) 106
Dumplings (RD) 107
Dumplings, herbed (RD) 107
Dumplings, sesame (RD) 107
Endive salad (RD) 46
Fig and ginger spread (RD) 114
Fish chowder (MD) 44
Fish patties (MD) 80
Fish stock 38
Fried rice special (RD) 62
Fruit, mixed sauté (RD) 87
Fruit sauté, seasonal (RD) 87
Fruit 'ice-cream' (RD) 83
Fruit jelly (RD) 90
Fruit milk shake (RD) 127
Fruit pikelets (RD) 112
Fruit salad chutney (RD) 115
Fruit scrolls (RD) 105
Fruit tarts (MD) 99
Fruit whip (RD) 125
Fruited jelly yoghurt (RD) 85
Fruited yoghurt (RD) 85
Garbanzo sauté (RD) 62
Garlic croutons (RD) 103
Ginger 'marmalade' (RD) 114
Ginger slice (RD) 94
Golden slice (RD) 91
Golden sultana tart (MD) 90
Golden tart (RD) 90
Goulash soup (MD) 38
Goulash soup and dumplings (MD) 38
Grape juice and apple toddy (MD) 128
Green tomato pickles (MD) 117
Hawaiian fish (MD) 80
Herbed chokos (RD) 62
Herbed damper (RD) 106
Herbed dumplings (RD) 107

Herbed pastry (RD) 109
Hot vegetable combo (RD) 63
Island rice salad (RD) 48
Jam tarts (RD) 99
Jellied beetroot (RD) 48
Kiwi fruit salad (RD) 51
Lean beef olives (MD) 72
Leek soup (RD) 41
Left-over soup (RD) 43
Lemon sago jelly (RD) 89
Lobster beef casserole (MD) 74
Mango chutney (MD) 116
Mango and pawpaw chutney (MD) 116
Marinade for meat (RD) 125
Mayonnaise, creamy (RD) 121
Mayonnaise 2 (RD) 121
Meat, poultry and fish 69–80
Minestrone soup (RD) 41
Mixed fruit sauté (RD) 87
Mixed vegetable salad (RD) 49
'Mock' turkey (RD) 117
Moist plain chestnut cake (RD) 100
More exchange cream (RD) 123, 124
Mushroom dip (RD) 123
Mushroom soufflé pie (RD) 58
Mustard and vinegar dressing (RD) 119
Onion croutons (RD) 103
Orange jelly (RD) 90
Orange muffins (RD) 105
Oriental salad (RD) 50
Pastry, citrus (RD) 109
Pastry, herbed (RD) 109
Pastry, plain (RD) 109
Pastry, potato (RD) 110
Pastry, sweet (RD) 109
Pastry, yeast (RD) 110
Peaches 'n cream (RD) 88
Pickled onions (MD) 118
Pikelets, basic (RD) 111; basic (RD) 111; date (MD) 111; fruit (RD) 112; raisin (MD) 111; sultana (MD) 111; sweet (RD) 111
Pineapple 'fritters' (RD) 86
Pineapple upside-down cake (RD) 86
Plain damper (RD) 106
Plain muffins (RD) 105

Plum sauce (MD) 124
Plum spread (RD) 114
Potato and tomato soup (RD) 40
Potato pastry (RD) 110
Quick tomato sauce (RD) 126
Quince and apple spread (RD) 115
Quince spread (RD) 114
Radish salad special (RD) 50
Raisin pikelets (RD) 111
Red cabbage sauté (RD) 57
Rich vegetable soup (RD) 42
Round beef paste (MD) 116
Salad toss supreme (RD) 51
Salads 45–52
Salmon paste (MD) 117
Salmon paste pinwheels (MD) 112
Scallop soup (RD) 44
Scalloped potatoes (RD) 57
Seasonal fruit sauté (RD) 87
'Seasoned' beef stew (MD) 74
Seasoned flour (RD) 125
Seasoned sweet sauce (RD) 126
Sesame dumplings (RD) 107
Snow peas Hawaiian style (RD) 58
Soup 37–44
Soy sauce dressing (RD) 121
Spaghetti with vegie sauce (RD) 59
Special French dressing (RD) 120
Spiced parsnips (RD) 60
Spiced vegetable medley (RD) 60
Spiced vinegar (MD) 118
Spicy carrot cake (MD) 97
Spinach-beef casserole (MD) 75
Spreads, chutneys and pastes 113–118
Sprouted bread (RD) 108
Sprouted brown rice scones (RD) 108
Steamed 'spread' pudding (RD) 88
Stock, beef 38; chicken 37; fish 38; vegetable 37
Strawberry milk shake (RD) 127
Stuffed pears (RD) 89
Stuffed pears with apricot and pineapple (RD) 89
Stuff 'Virginia' roast (MD) 72
Sultana pikelets (MD) 111
Sultana slice (MD) 95
Summer punch (MD) 128
Sunshine vegetable medley (RD) 60
Sunshine island rice salad (MD) 49
Swede and carrot special (RD) 65
Sweet more exchange cream (RD) 123
Sweet pastry (RD) 109
Sweet pikelets (RD) 111
Sweet scrolls (MD) 105
Sweet 'n sour sauce (RD) 123
Sweet 'n sour vegies (RD) 64
Sweet 'n sour vegies and rice (RD) 64
Sweet vegetable sauté (RD) 64
Tarragon dressing (RD) 119
Thousand island dressing (RD) 120
Tomato and cabbage soup (RD) 49
Tomato baked beans (RD) 66
Tomato cocktail (RD) 128
Tomato-flavoured left-over soup (RD) 43
Tomato lentil special (RD) 67
Tomato salad (RD) 48
Tomato spread (RD) 115
Tomato spread with grape juice (MD) 115
Tomatoes, hot spiced (RD) 67
Tomatoes with chicken (MD) 77
Tuna patties (MD) 80
Vanilla custard (RD) 81
Vanilla 'ice-cream' (RD) 83
Vegetable cheese pie (RD) 66
Vegetable juice quencher (RD) 128
Vegetable stock 37
Vegetables 53–68
Waldorf salad (MD) 52
Water chestnuts and beans (RD) 65
Wheat free 'eggless' Christmas cake (MD) 96
Wheat salad (RD) 51
White sauce (RD) 122
Yeast pastry (RD) 110
Zucchini, new potato and adzuki bean salad (RD) 47